HOW TO WRITE A WINNING UCAS PERSONAL STATEMENT

Contents

PREFACE

ince the second edition of this book was published much has changed again in the higher education world, with the arrival of £9,000 tuition fees and expansion of the number of courses on offer. We have also seen the number of overseas applicants to UK universities increase, and the number of UK applicants to European universities rise simultaneously. The A level system was overhauled by the Coalition government, elected in 2010, so that from 2015, in a rolling programme, all A level courses will be taught in a linear format; the old AS to A2 model will be phased out by 2017. Some students will still be taking AS, but maybe not so many. If they do take them, the results will be in their application and available for universities to use in their assessment. Where they are not available, universities and colleges may use GCSE results to assess performance. The number of pupils taking the Cambridge Pre-U and the International Baccalaureate (IB) in the UK is also rising, slowly but surely.

The need for a new edition to this book is now imperative, not only to reflect these and other changes, but to update the information about courses. It remains the case that the personal statement is a pivotal part of any good application and, for that reason, the advice in this book has been updated to ensure that all the 'inside information' is current and accurate. This remains this book's unique selling point – it is one of a few books that have gone direct to the universities for an inside look at exactly what they look for in a good applicant. The subject profiles are written by university admissions officers speaking, as it were, directly to a potential applicant. All of these sections have been revised to reflect the current situation. The frequently asked questions have also been updated. These include an answer to a question about the new UCAS Tariffs. They have had to be changed for courses starting in 2017. This is to reflect the change to AS and A2 and the weighting that they are given as decoupled courses. It sounds complicated, but it is not really.

The essential principles of success remain the same. If you work hard at what you enjoy, take care to present yourself enthusiastically and articulately, and take the time to think about what you want from life, you will not go far wrong. Applying to university is not an exact science. Choices about *where* to study, *what* to study and *whether* to study are essentially personal.

You therefore need to be informed. This information also needs to be informed by current experience and reality, not 'what it was like in my day'!

My own views have been coloured by working at one the UK's ancient schools, Christ's Hospital, for the last twenty years. Over the last two decades I have advised many hundreds of students applying to universities throughout the UK and, increasingly, overseas too. Although Christ's Hospital is an independent school, with able students, it remains true to its ancient mission and offers the vast majority of its pupils means-tested bursaries and scholarships. These pupils mix happily with full fee-paying boarders and day pupils, leading to an eclectic mix of UK and international students from across the social spectrum. Some applicants are the first to apply to university from their immediate family. Others are sons or daughters of Oxford graduates who bring their own unique problems to solve!

I know about the full range of issues that can arise when making an application. I also know what the parents feel too! The personal statement is, for many applicants, the scariest part of the application. It need not be so!

Ian Stannard
January 2016

ACKNOWLEDGEMENTS

riting a book of this length and complexity is no easy task and I am grateful to the many people who have helped me compose it originally and update it here for the third time.

I am grateful first of all to Della Oliver and the team at Trotman who felt it worthwhile to launch a third edition, suitably updated and revised. Her support in the editing process has been excellent.

I am grateful, too, for the support and advice I have had from Godfrey Cooper, who has read the text many times, done research for me and helped to proof-read the revisions.

Thanks, too, to all the admissions tutors from the universities who have given their time to revise the profiles to ensure that the information is accurate, websites are current and personal statement advice is pertinent to new applicants. Also, to the select bunch of pupils at Christ's Hospital who were so helpful in providing a critical appraisal of what I wrote, suggesting improvements along the way.

Finally, thank you to my wife and children who have had to put up with me hogging the computer and talking to people for hours on the phone!

PART ONE

THE PROCESS, A STEP-BY-STEP GUIDE

INTRODUCTION

> ❝ The first thing you must remember is that your personal statement will probably be the only opportunity you get to 'talk' directly to the Admissions Selector on the programme you want to study. It is therefore vitally important that you make this statement as effective as possible! ❞
> **DURHAM UNIVERSITY**

The personal statement is probably the most important piece of writing that most students aiming to gain entry to higher education will complete outside of an examination hall. In an increasingly competitive marketplace, the supply of good courses in many areas of study is outstripped by demand. The result is that, for some highly competitive courses, the number of applicants can exceed supply by ten times.

Most universities do not interview candidates. You are unlikely to be interviewed unless you are applying to Oxford, Cambridge, veterinary science, medicine or a profession-allied-to-medicine course (dentistry, nursing, physiotherapy). Instead, they rely principally on four pieces of information when deciding whether to offer the applicant a place:

1   the student's academic record so far (GCSE or alternative results) and their current academic profile – are they studying A levels, International Baccalaureate or an equivalent qualification such as the Pre-U? This may become more important as we move away from the AS exams.

2   the student's personal statement

3   the academic reference provided by the school or college

4   the predicted grades that the school or college provides. Predictions are provided by the school and are normally based on the pupil's most recent performance in class or in mock exams.

My experience of talking to many current admissions tutors is that they look first at the academic record and second at the personal statement. They do look carefully at predicted grades and the academic reference, but increasingly they base their decision on the actual GCSE grades achieved to date and the quality of the personal statement.

Note: The loss of their ability to look at completed AS grades for some students will make their job harder and increase the significance of the predicted grades and the pupils' GCSE results. Some universities use GCSE results as a first sift, removing applicants whose grades fall below a certain threshold.

Many schools now write references that are somewhat bland. In the past, they were confidential, so referees could be honest with admissions tutors. Today they are not, and many schools feel unable to be as candid. For that reason, their usefulness is diminished.

Universities still read the references, but they are concerned about their usefulness. This is highlighted by the University of Leicester, who have a few useful comments to make that all applicants can bear in mind when talking to the school or college about a reference.

Here is a selection of suggestions direct from Leicester's admissions tutors.

> It may seem like an obvious point to make, but many references are plain and generic and could have been written about anyone. I have also seen the occasional one where the teacher has forgotten to change the name of the student from the last time they used the reference.
>
> **DR DANIEL ATTENBOROUGH (LAW)**

> Include something on how well this student might be suited to studying in HE (not just in academic terms but in terms of independence, organisation, etc.). Try to avoid repetition/overlap with personal statement – the reference should 'add value' to the application.
>
> **DR PATRICK WHITE (SOCIOLOGY)**

> Detailed prediction for each subject is good. 'If they work hard could achieve a B'; 'should easily achieve a

B' – this gives a stronger feel for the likely grades. References that talk about the course, not the student are not so useful.**"**
DAWN WEDD (ECONOMICS)

RECORD NUMBERS APPLYING!

University applications have reached record levels. More than 593,000 people applied to start courses in the autumn of 2016, up 2% on 2015. The rise in applications is across the board, with increasing applications from all regions of England and Northern Ireland. The gender gap is also growing, with women driving the increasing demand for places. In England, 35% of 18-year-olds are applying to university, but below this headline figure is evidence to suggest that the majority of these applicants are now women.

Recent figures also show that the demand from the EU and USA for UK courses is rising. It is a myth that these applicants will impact on UK applicants – most UK universities have quotas of overseas students to ensure that the mix remains predominantly UK based. But this is not always the case, so do look at this carefully. One UK university with a very high non-UK student base is the London School of Economics.

All these figures indicate that, despite rising fees, the demand remains buoyant.

WIDENING PARTICIPATION – ACCESS TO UNIVERSITY FOR UNDER-REPRESENTED GROUPS

Where work still needs to be done is in the widening participation area. All universities have made great progress in encouraging applications from applicants in disadvantaged groups. However, it is still the case that applicants from middle-class backgrounds are twice as common as those from lower socio-economic groups. There are many reasons for this, but this is not the time or the place to discuss them.

King's College London is one of many universities that actively seek applicants from groups that are not as well represented in UK universities. The aim behind widening participation is to ensure that student bodies at universities reflect the diversity represented in wider society.

King's College's website refers to the following groups whom they want to see apply:

- young people from low-income backgrounds
- young people from low-participation neighbourhoods (where very few people go on to higher education)
- young people whose parents did not go to university

- young people in or leaving care
- young people living with a disability
- young people from an ethnic minority
- those returning to learning as mature students.

So, if you are an applicant who meets one of the above criteria, then you are more likely to be offered a place! Please also make this clear in your personal statement and ask the school to reinforce this in their reference. They really do actively look for applicants who could be just like you – so don't hide, and be bold. Sometimes the grades required of such applicants are lower to reflect this. This is controversial, but it is a reality that most universities will admit to when cornered!

'SO WHAT?' YOU MAY ASK

Well – it is hard to get a place at a good university and it appears to be getting harder every year. Therefore, it is vital that you follow these basic rules of thumb:

1 **Your UCAS application must be handed in on time and be free from errors**. There is a school of thought that says that an early application gives an applicant an edge. This depends on the policy of the university. Some offer places throughout the application cycle (normally September to mid-January) and others operate what is known as a 'gathered field' approach and wait until the closing date. However, in my experience an early application cannot do any harm. Don't forget that Oxford, Cambridge, medical, veterinary and dental applications must be completed by 15 October.

2 **Your personal statement must sell you in a way that is compelling, engaging and well informed**. A lazy approach to this key document is fatal, particularly if you are applying to a course that is oversubscribed. A busy admissions tutor is looking for a reason to reject you as much as to offer you a place! In the real world, tutors will face a large pile of applications knowing that they are going to have to whittle them down to a shortlist. Don't give them an excuse to bin yours because of a poor statement.

3 **Your reasons for applying must be good**. Your statement must point to evidence that indicates that you understand the course content and have the skills to thrive in their department. This means taking time to do the research properly before doing anything else. I cannot emphasise this enough. Make an informed choice about what to study and where. Don't just do what your parents want or your friends are doing. That is fatal and potentially very expensive.

It is a myth that the personal statement is the hardest thing to write, although in my experience it is what causes 50% of the heartache. The other 50% is deciding what to study and where. Don't just go somewhere because of the name of the university. Again, that is fatal. Look instead at the employability of graduates from those courses. In the end, that is as important. Will you get a job at the end?

Other key factors to consider are the following:

- Location and cost of living – can you really afford to live there? London is great, but very expensive, so take care to think about budgeting. Some students now consider it wise to live near enough to home or a family member that they can live with in the second or third year. This will potentially save you £6,000 when you take into consideration the cost of housing, food and amenities.
- Accommodation – what is on offer? How expensive is it? Can they offer it to all undergraduates in the first year? What about in subsequent years? I would recommend that you live in a hall of residence in the first year as it is a great way of making friends.
- What is it about the course that attracts you? Be specific and expect to articulate this in the statement.
- What sports or other facilities do they have?
- Is it a campus or non-campus university? They are very different in feel.
- Have you visited the university? Only crazy people apply to live and study for three years at a university without actually having had a good look around. Can you imagine living there?
- What about the local area? Does it feel safe? Is it somewhere you might be able to get a job locally?
- What welfare facilities do they offer? Do they have a good Students' Union? Is there good special educational needs provision?
- Do they offer bursaries or hardship funds? How do you apply for them?
- What is the quality of the teaching like? What do existing students think about the course? This is information that you will get from the 'independent' websites that collate information about universities or from books such as the *Times University Guide*.

Making decisions is tough, and for many of you this is the first time you will be making a major educational decision without your parents being at the centre of the process. You should consider their advice, together with the advice gained from books such as this, from your teachers, from online university prospectuses and from other sources of information.

Do not despair! I am a strong believer in the phrase 'Keep It Simple, Stupid', or KISS for short! This is the purpose of this book. I aim to make the process of deciding what and where to study and writing your statement less painful and more fulfilling. I have worked with thousands of students applying to universities all over the UK and have read more personal statements than I care to admit. If you follow the advice in this book, you will be well on the way to producing a statement and application that will win you the offer you want.

CHAPTER ONE

NO SHORT CUTS:
FIRST DO YOUR RESEARCH!

 You cannot write a good personal statement in isolation. The information you need to write it well is gathered only by careful research. This takes time, but it is time well spent.

Think of the **what**, **why** and **where** questions that we often ask ourselves.

You need to find out *what you want to study*, *why this subject motivates you* and then consider *where you want to study*. A common theme in all the conversations I have had with admissions tutors is that four things are vital:

- that you know what you really want from a university course
- that you can sell your enthusiasm for the subject clearly and with confidence
- that you know what academic grades the departments are looking for – be brave but also realistic
- that the location you choose suits your personality and wider interests.

This is where the academic profiles found later in the book will be so useful to you.

Each one takes a different subject area and lets you know what studying that subject may be like, the qualities admissions tutors look for in a good candidate, what to write and what to avoid in your personal statement and other tips to make your application stand out from the crowd. These were all written in collaboration with real admissions tutors and therefore do represent an inside guide to how to impress a busy academic tutor.

Here are some extracts about a range of subjects to whet your appetite!

This is what a tutor at Queen Mary University of London has to say about the skills or attributes that they look for in a good applicant for English:

> 66 Admissions tutors will always consider the level of attainment in GCSEs and predicted grades for A levels first of all. Many English courses now demand very high grades, simply due to supply and demand. It is not at all uncommon for candidates to be made offers of AAB or higher. Equally, it is not unusual for candidates to be rejected from one or more of their preferred universities. However, it is also possible to get into English courses with lower grades. Do your research carefully! 99

The personal statement and school reference are then read for any signs that interest in English is not just confined to A level. Tutors would hope to see indications of long-standing enjoyment, and an understanding that English at university will not be like three more years of A level English, but will be more demanding and unpredictable. They want to see evidence of wide reading and an appreciation of different literary genres.

This is shown in this quote from an admissions tutor from Swansea University.

> 66 A succinct and focused statement that: specifies the kind of books you enjoy, details the specific aspects of literary study that appeal to you and, crucially, why … It is vital that it is written in good English (naturally), using correct punctuation and uncomplicated syntax. Avoid deep and meaningful philosophical statements, overlong sentences and incorrect punctuation … Good applicants demonstrate excellent academic potential, demonstrated by their strong A level or equivalent grades, and enthusiasm for further study. They show good time management and teamwork skills; the ability to manage independent study successfully and to work co-operatively in seminars and group projects. 99

All this information needs to be included in your personal statement or academic reference!

Here are some comments on what makes for a good personal statement for a potential physiotherapist, from an admissions tutor at the University of Brighton.

> It's really helpful if you have observed some physiotherapy sessions, to briefly describe your experience and explain why you would like to study it. You really need to describe something more varied than a personal experience of receiving physiotherapy – which shows that you have made an effort to see different aspects of physiotherapy – or at least have plans to broaden your understanding. Many departments do not look favourably at an overemphasis on sport. Most physiotherapists work in hospital settings and do not get involved in any form of sports-related injury or rehabilitation.

> It's always good to hear about your activities beyond the academic, particularly if you are interested in continuing them at university. Try to show a range of interests other than sport. We are interested in music, drama and other extra-curricular pursuits, especially if they show evidence of individual leadership or teamwork skills. If you have had a job or done voluntary work make sure you explain something positive about the experience of interacting with people.

> Try to find a balance between self-promotion, explaining your recent experiences of work, social activities and school achievements. Overemphasis on any of these elements can skew your statement.

SUMMARY

A good personal statement is one that is written at the end of an exhaustive research process. Students who are right for the course, who have understood the demands of the subject and are ready to take on the challenge, write winning personal statements.

Weak personal statements are under-prepared, written in a hurry and without the zeal that is evident when applicants know what they want and promote themselves with confidence.

Before you even start to write your personal statement you need to ask yourself some searching questions and be prepared to work hard to find the answers. Good applications are often successful applications, and successful applications are informed and enhanced by good research.

Too many students drop out of university in their first year or change their course when they arrive, because they were poorly informed from the outset.

One good way to start is to answer the following questions – make notes that you can refer back to later when you start to draft your statement.

QUESTIONS TO ASK YOURSELF

Why do you want to study that subject and what evidence do you have that your interest is real and not superficial?

This is a key component of the first plan of your personal statement.

Where do you want to study and why?

Admissions tutors want to know that your reasons for studying a subject at their university are based on good grounds. Do you understand the demands of the course and of the type of teaching and learning styles that you will encounter? This is something that ought to be addressed in a statement.

What do you know about the skills and attributes that the admissions tutor is looking for and how will you convince them that you possess these key skills?

Emphasise these skills in your statement.

What evidence can you provide that supports your interest? This evidence must be more than just a list of what you have done at A level.

A good personal statement will show evidence of wider reading or participation in activities that support and extend your knowledge and understanding of the course you have applied for.

What do admissions tutors in your area of interest look for in a good statement?	Go to the profile section first and, if in doubt, email or telephone a tutor at a local university for advice. They are keen to hear from potential applicants, particularly those local to the university.
What have your studies so far taught you about the course you hope to apply for – for instance, if applying to read Chemistry, what have you done at A level or equivalent that sparked your interest?	This is another key part of your personal statement and may be included in the first or second section.

As you can see, there is a lot to think about before you start your first draft. I will start by asking you some questions about your motivation to study; your subject interests and what skills you have that you hope to extend at university. I will ask some searching questions that you may like to discuss with your family, friends or schoolteachers. I will also point you in the direction of some excellent books, websites and organisations that may help you in this initial process.

Only when you can answer all these questions are you ready to start the drafting stage. I suggest that you divide your statement into three distinct parts, working on each one and then drawing them together at the end. Each part has its own emphasis and importance, and a chapter of the book is devoted to each one in turn.

We start with some advice about research – why to do it, how to do it and where to look for expert help and guidance.

CHAPTER TWO

WHY GO TO UNIVERSITY IN THE FIRST PLACE?

In your parents' lifetime, the number of students in full-time education post-18 has risen significantly. In the 1980s, less than 20% of the population attended a British university. That figure is now nearly 45%. The cost of university has also risen from zero to £9,000 per year in tuition fees. Loans have largely replaced grants and the average student can now expect to leave university with debts over £40,000. However, this is not something to worry about unduly.

The debt is to the government, not a bank or credit card agency. The interest rates are much lower than for commercial loans and the risk to you is lower too. For instance, a graduate earning £26,000 and with a student debt of £43,500 would pay back £30 a month until the debt was paid off. This figure changes year on year, and would increase as your income increased, but the point I am making is that debt should not deter you from starting a course, regardless of your social situation.

SO WHY GO?

Essentially, the reasons for this are varied and the following are some of the factors that students I have worked with have come up with.

- **To get a good job**. Most professional careers now have a recognised graduate entry route. Although it is not imperative to get a degree in order to get a good job, there is an assumption that graduates are more likely to be employed. Of course, once you start your career, your success or otherwise will depend on your ability to do the job. A degree is just the key to the door; it does not always guarantee that you will enjoy accelerated promotion.
- **Note:** Many top firms are now reintroducing their A level entry routes to cater for an increase in demand. These can sometimes be referred to as Apprenticeships. This is not something to ignore, so look at this possibility sensibly too. One good example of this is accountancy firms, who are happy to recruit able A level students and train them on the job. Top firms expect top grades, though!

- **To please my parents**. Many parents live vicariously through their children. In my experience they vary in their approach. Some parents are too pushy and expect their children to go to university, as this was their own experience. This is particularly true of parents who expect their child to get a place at Oxbridge or medical school. Others are equally forceful about the need to get a degree, especially if, as non-graduates themselves, they realise the advantages of a degree in career progression. Make sure you talk to your parents about the A level entry routes to good careers too – just to ensure that everyone is informed.
- **All my friends are applying**. This is another powerful pull towards university. This is particularly the case when the student's friends all aspire to higher education.
- **To better myself**. This group of students want to go to university to help them enjoy a better life than their parents were able to give them. This is called social mobility and is high on the government's agenda. Evidence does suggest that the most successful students at university will often be those who had to fight hard to get in, perhaps against the odds, for a variety of social or educational reasons. The widening participation model was established to work with and encourage this cohort of students.
- **My chosen career requires me to graduate**. Many degree courses, for example medicine, nursing, engineering, physiotherapy and veterinary science, are vocational and a degree qualification is an essential first step. This is not likely to change in the short term.
- **To make more money**. This is the most mercenary of all the motives but probably lies at the heart of most students' thoughts when they are contemplating three more years in education.

Recent research indicates that, taking into account the tuition fees, student loans and taxation on earnings over a lifetime, as a man you'll have earned an additional 28% more (£168k over a working lifetime) on average, as compared with someone with a similar background who didn't go to university. For a woman, it's an additional 52% (£252k over a working lifetime), as there tends to be a bigger difference between the types of jobs women do as graduates, as compared with non-graduates.

But it's effort that matters most. A 'good' degree (First or 2.i) means significantly higher returns than for lower degree classes (by £76k for men and £85k for women, on average). And good degrees are earned, not given.

PAUSE FOR THOUGHT – TIME TO ASK YOURSELF SOME IMPORTANT QUESTIONS!

Read the following questions. Take notes of your answers to refer back to later on. These questions are often best debated with friends, family and teachers at your school or college. Don't be afraid to ask the opinions of others to help inform your own opinion.

These are all important questions to answer **before** you start to write your personal statement. They force you to look at yourself critically and assess the real reason why you want to stay in full-time education – or perhaps not, and take some time out.

Do you look forward to leaving school and beginning higher education?

Leaving school can be an exciting and scary prospect. The certainties of school and college life are lost. You are used to a group of friends that you may have known for years, rules that you understand (even if you hate them!), teachers whom you understand how to manipulate and teaching styles that you are used to. Starting again in a new institution, away from home for the first time and with all the bills to pay yourself can be daunting! Do not be afraid to express these fears and talk them through. You are not alone – far from it!

Do you want to continue to study a subject that you are studying at school or college?

Most students study a subject at university that is in some way linked to their educational choices post-16. Even if you are not studying the subject directly, such as English, chemistry or maths, many will choose a discipline that builds on skills learnt at A level (or their equivalent); for instance, biochemistry or nursing, which both build on science skills learnt at school. This is important to consider when choosing the course. Clearly, this is not always the case and many people go on to study subjects such as psychology, history of art, criminology, law or archaeology without actually ever having studied these at school.

How will you show this transfer of skills in your personal statement?

Going to university is also the opportunity to do other subjects that you are interested to explore but may not have done before. Subjects such as archaeology, Classics, philosophy, law, podiatry and management are open to you in a way that they may not have been at school. Here, the admissions tutors are not looking for evidence of existing A level knowledge, just potential and latent interest. For example, the Classics tutor at King's College London makes it clear that they do not look for Classics or Latin at A level, but rather for skills picked up in most humanities or language courses.

> As a good Classics (etc.) applicant you will have the same general skills and attributes as any good humanities prospect: enthusiasm, self-motivation, a desire to learn, an appetite both for different perspectives and for challenging questions. The King's College London admissions team hope to see applicants who enjoy independently exploring new topics, whether in the

library, the museum or the field; people who want to engage with new problems and techniques, and to get behind the clichés of mass-media versions of ancient myth and conflict. 🥚

Do you want to live away from home?

Unlike in mainland Europe, UK students have traditionally moved away from home to study post-18. This is a trend that seems to be in modest decline, with an increasing number of students choosing to live in their home town. This is particularly true of undergraduates from poorer families with little history of higher education. Reasons for this vary, but the financial advantage of home life is one major factor. It can cost in excess of £140 per week to live in a hall of residence in London, which is a major expense for most students starting a degree course. That being said, my strong advice is to live in halls of residence in the first year if at all possible. Living at home in the first year can make it hard to make friends and will cramp your style!

Are you willing to pay for this opportunity and what is your attitude to debt?

It is not cheap to study at university. There are a number of costs that need to be met and for most students there is a shortfall between the income they receive from grants, bursaries and loans and the total cost of living. However, the advantages of a university degree are significant and money should not put anyone off giving it a try. Do consider the cost of living when looking at location. It is far more expensive to live and study in London than in Hull! You will learn to live in debt as a student but this is quite manageable if you follow some simple tips.

- Learn to budget. Look at your outgoings (spending habits) and look at your income; as much as possible, try not to leave too big a gap between the two.
- Avoid credit cards and store cards. These are often a disaster for students and can lead to major problems, including court action, if you cannot make the payments. I know more than one former student who cannot get a mortgage now because of credit card debt when they were at university. This is real life now, not school rules and detentions!
- Expect to have to get a job in term time and in the holidays. This is true unless you are applying to Cambridge or Oxford, where the short terms and high workload make it inadvisable to get a part-time job in term time. Colleges have funds to help students in need.
- Keep a check on your spending on luxuries, including alcohol and fast food. Try to learn to cook for yourself, as this is almost always cheaper than precooked microwave meals. It is also sometimes cheaper to live in catered halls as the food is provided for you. As long as you eat it, this will cut your bills!

- Avoid unnecessary expenditure such as car insurance. Cars at university rarely make sense unless absolutely necessary. You become a taxi service!
- Make sure that you have personal insurance away from home and that you get a TV licence if you have a TV in your room. A hefty bill after a fire, or a fine from TV licensing is not in most students' budget plans!

A small number of my former students have made all these mistakes in the last few years. For good advice, consult one of the many good guides to student money available in bookshops or online.

Are you an independent learner?

All my research indicates that the ability to show evidence of this skill is vital. If possible, mention your independent learning in the personal statement, with evidence to support your claim.

The learning and teaching style at school is very different from that at university. There is a lot more emphasis on personal learning and initiative. This lack of direction and teacher contact is often a major source of disappointment for new undergraduates. Admissions tutors are looking for evidence in the personal statement that you have the drive and personal initiative to cope in this sort of environment. To give you an example, here is an extract from a profile written by admissions tutors at the University of Surrey and Durham University, both of which admit students into modern language courses.

" Most language courses are taught using a variety of different methods. Some lectures are conducted either in English or a foreign language. These would normally be lectures to support modules in history, business or law, for instance. They would also see students in small seminars, where the language is spoken and discussions take place about literature, politics or current affairs. Students are also encouraged to give presentations in the foreign language. Departments also use language laboratories and audio-visual material, from films to foreign documentaries. In most departments teaching methods therefore aim to promote 'student-centred learning'. This means that they encourage you to be responsible for your own learning and for the organisation of your work, and to set high standards and goals, such as near-native competence in your target languages. The role of the teacher in this process is to encourage and support you, to guide your learning and to engage in an exchange of ideas with you. **"**

Are you clear about the career you want to pursue and do you expect to have to get a degree to start this career?

Some careers such as medicine, architecture, nursing and engineering require vocational degree qualifications. Your personal statement needs to show evidence of your commitment to these careers before you apply. Have you completed work experience and, if so, what did you learn? Have you taken time to speak to practitioners or even worked for companies in that industry?

Do not worry if you do not have a clear idea of what career to pursue. Most graduates use their degree to get them an interview on a graduate scheme – they do not actually use the subject matter again. I got onto a leading bank's graduate scheme with a degree in theology and philosophy!

What reasons might you have for not going to university?

Think about what you might do if you do not go to university. Are you going for good reasons? If not, and you are not committed to a course, this will show in the personal statement as it will lack clarity and personal enthusiasm.

Should students from widening participation groups indicate this on their application form or personal statement?

This struck me as an important question to ask the admissions tutors who collaborated with me on this book. If there was an advantage to be had if you were considered a widening participation applicant, then your status ought to be made clear in your personal statement or academic reference.

The answers we received from the universities varied. Some were adamant that they did not look at the socio-economic group at all. They simply accepted pupils based on academic potential, regardless of their background.

Others did look at the school to see what success it had in sending students to university and this may favour a borderline candidate. A good candidate from a school with little or no history of sending students to university would be given extra credit.

Others advise you to be explicit if you are from a group that meets the widening participation criteria. You should mention it if you are the first in your immediate family to attend university or that you are in a family that is economically disadvantaged. This is perhaps best done in the final paragraph of your personal statement, and this is what I encourage my students to do. The school should also allude to this in its academic reference.

The following are direct quotes from a couple of university departments.

> **‟** The Institute of Archaeology very much supports the widening participation agenda, and has undertaken numerous activities to encourage applicants from a wide range of backgrounds, including taster days, master classes, and events in National Archaeology Week. As a discipline, archaeology has traditionally attracted a very broad spectrum of applicants, including a high proportion of adult learners. **”**
> **UNIVERSITY COLLEGE LONDON**

> **‟** We've always encouraged widening participation and invite a large proportion of people who apply to us to come to our auditions. It can be helpful to see an explanation that someone has not had the opportunities to take part in a range of acting roles simply because of their personal circumstances. This would not in any way debar from audition. **”**
> **THE LIVERPOOL INSTITUTE FOR PERFORMING ARTS**

All admissions tutors recognised that some issues that the applicant may want to raise, and that are pertinent to the application, may be too private for a public document. Such issues could be expressed in a letter sent directly to the admissions office of each university. Too few applicants disclose this sort of information and this is detrimental to them and their application. All letters sent would be considered in confidence. Such letters should be supported by medical opinion, social work reports or other third-party agency testimonials, where such support is appropriate. (*You are advised not to mention anything in your personal statement that you would not want to be read by too many people – this is the beauty of the supplementary letter*.)

Note: these letters should not be sent until after the application has been sent to UCAS and the applicant has received the letter of confirmation from UCAS.

Do you have any disability or special needs?

All UK universities welcome knowing if a student has a diagnosed disability or special need. Such students will not be prejudiced in any way; it will help the universities to understand your results in context, and money is often available to support you at university.

From 2009, applicants were obliged to enter details about any disability or special need on the UCAS form, even if it were simply to confirm that they had none. Be prepared to provide evidence from a doctor or educational psychologist if required. There is no stigma attached to such claims.

WHAT HAPPENS NEXT?

The final stage of research before you start to write your personal statement considers the two most important questions:

1   What should I study?

2   Where should I study?

CHAPTER THREE
WHAT COURSE TO STUDY AND WHERE?

Before you start making an application and writing your personal statement, I want you to take some time to consider what it is you want to study, and where. Many students just 'end up' at university without giving any serious thought to the nature of the course and location.

First, write down your answers to the following questions – you will refer to them again when you start to write your statement.

- List at least four reasons why it is important for you to go to university (in order of importance to you).
- Have you a particular subject or course in mind?
- If your answer is 'yes', can you write down some of the factors that influence your choice? In particular, think about the skills or attributes you possess that support your interest.
- If your answer is 'no', can you at least isolate the skills you have that you want to enhance and develop at university. These might include literary, mechanical, design, mathematical, artistic or sporting skills. It is clearly worthwhile playing to your strengths.
- Have you a clear career path in mind? Will this career require any qualifications that you can gain at university or college?
- Do you want to live near your home or would you be willing to move a long way away? Is location an important factor in your decision making?
- Do you have a university in mind as your first choice? If so, what reasons can you give that support this choice? Do you know whether the course requirements meet your expectations and academic potential?
- What about the other choices? You can apply to up to five in total, unless you are applying to medical, dental or veterinary school, where you can apply to only four.

WHAT TO STUDY?
You need to really know yourself and know the departments you hope to persuade to accept you. You must do your research and make it clear in the application and your personal

statement that you have done this thoroughly. As you will see in the academic profiles, admissions tutors often refer to students applying with little understanding of the demands of the course. Their applications and personal statements are more often than not consigned to the reject pile.

To research universities effectively, you can do the following.

- Use the excellent UCAS website (www.ucas.com) – this is for many people the first port of call. Its course search function contains links to all the courses on offer in the UK.
- Read carefully the websites of the universities that you have shortlisted and visit the universities wherever possible. University websites are updated weekly and now you can often see webcams, video presentations from departments and virtual tours of campus accommodation. This is all much more useful than the old paper prospectuses.
- Look at the books recommended in this book – most can be found in a library if you do not wish to pay for your own copy. The reading lists have all been updated for this new edition and contain both reference books and subject-specific guides. There are also book suggestions at the end of each academic profile.

THE UCAS WEBSITE

The UCAS website (www.ucas.com) is an excellent site, full of useful advice. It has a comprehensive course search facility that allows you to access every course that is offered in the UK through the UCAS system. It allows you to compare courses and find out more about the nature of the courses.

Do use the course search facility for an initial sift through what's available. Look at the 'entry profiles' that have been compiled by all the universities. These give a good insight into what they are looking for in a good candidate.

WHERE TO STUDY?

There will be many reasons why it is either appropriate or inappropriate to apply to a particular university – these include academic grade expectation, cost of living, course content, proximity to home, graduate employment prospects and location (rural vs. urban; campus vs. non-campus). All these factors need to be teased out before you start to write your statement.

My students often ask what is the right university for them. Here is my answer, which I trust will help you to compose your own. In short, the best university is the one that best suits the individual student! It is the university that offers you:

- a course that is interesting – make sure that you apply for a course that meets your needs and that, equally, you do not apply for a course that does not. A Warwick admissions tutor remarked to me recently that he was amazed at the number of students who simply applied because of the 'name' of the university, rather than because the course suited them. Such applicants often failed to gain a place, as it was clear that they had not done their research.
- a good quality of teaching – look at the information you can find on the excellent Guardian University Guide website. This is free and updated annually. League tables are not the be all and end all, but they are good places to start.
- a favourable geographical location. Think about proximity to home, for instance.
- a realistic and achievable conditional offer – it is clearly not appropriate to apply for a course where the expected grades significantly exceed your grade predictions and previous academic record. The following advice from the University of Leicester to school teachers who are guiding applicants is worth looking at.

> ❝ Be honest with your students! Students need to be realistic when looking at course requirements. Many universities make conditional offers to students based, in part, on their predicted grades and so it is important that these grades are achievable by the student. Students who have over-estimated grades often miss their conditional offer requirements and then have the stress of entering Clearing. ❞

- a good graduate employment record – very important, particularly in the current economic climate. All universities publish this information.
- a range of excellent facilities – not least, affordable accommodation. Do check carefully how much the accommodation on offer will cost. Also check if they want you to leave at Christmas and Easter. This can affect costs significantly. Finally, see if they offer both catered and self-catering accommodation; there is a market for both.

Choosing a course that is interesting and has good-quality teaching

When doing your research, the following tips are useful.

- Check the research and teaching rating for the relevant course on the latest league tables. League tables are a good place to start, but do not reject those whose research rating is lower than 4. Tables should be treated as starting points, not ends in themselves.
- The premier league of the British university system includes the Russell Group universities. They are the ones with the best research ratings overall, the best

reputation with employers (normally) and highest kudos. Most commentators suggest that the following are in the 'premier' league (not all in the Russell Group): Bath, Birmingham, Bristol, Cambridge, Cardiff, Durham, Edinburgh, Exeter, Glasgow, Imperial, King's London, Leeds, Liverpool, LSE, Manchester, Newcastle, Nottingham, Oxford, Sheffield, Southampton, St Andrew's, Sussex, UCL, Warwick and York.

- The best course for you may not be at one of the so-called 'best' universities. You need to consider other factors, most notably employment prospects, course content and location. For instance, City has a world-class banking and journalism course and Brunel is renowned internationally for its design degrees. Other rising stars include Surrey, Aston and Leicester.

- Online prospectuses are also first-rate information guides and are updated before each admissions cycle. They can often provide more up-to-date information than the expensive-looking paper versions. Many have useful videos and links to sites that help you to make informed choices. Look at the accommodation and welfare information too. What is the cost of accommodation, what bursaries are on offer and how do they cater for students with particular learning needs?

- Some independent sites are also being developed. One such site is www.whatuni. com. These provide a one-stop shop and are a good place to start. They also provide details of open days and taster events. These 'taster' events are particularly useful when preparing the first part of your personal statement. Both UNISTATS (unistats.direct.gov.uk) and Which? University (www.university.which.co.uk) publish detailed information on the relative merits of different courses and institutions, based on feedback provided by current and previous students, as well as data from sources such as the Higher Education Statistics Agency (HESA).

TO SUMMARISE

FACTORS IN YOUR CHOICE

The right geographical location	Do you want to live away from home? There are personal development factors to be gained by living away from home and this can prove significant when seeking a job.
An offer that realistically you are going to achieve	You need to balance optimism with pragmatism. Ask yourself what you really expect to achieve and what evidence from past performance you can point to in your personal statement and academic reference to support this. There is no point applying for a course that you cannot reasonably expect to get into with your predictions or subject profile.

A good employment record for recent graduates	If you are clear about what you want to do after university, your chosen subject must provide a suitable basis for that career.
A range of excellent facilities, including accommodation	The facilities offered by all universities are similar; they will all have a library, a sports hall and a careers service. However, if you require a specialised facility, then this is a factor to consider. A climber is not advised to go to East Anglia if he or she wants access to mountains!

Now it is time to get started on the writing bit!

CHAPTER FOUR
YOUR PERSONAL STATEMENT: GETTING STARTED

Your personal statement is, I believe, the most important piece of writing that you will complete outside of the examination hall. For that reason alone, it is vital to take the time to get it right. Most universities in the UK do not have the resources to select via interview. Cambridge interviews almost all candidates whose applications are considered worthy of further exploration; Oxford does the same in some subjects but 'deselects' between 20% and 25% of applicants for some subjects. Other universities do interview, but this tends to be for highly competitive courses, vocational courses such as medicine, veterinary science or nursing. Artists and architecture applicants are often interviewed to examine their portfolio, and drama and music students should expect an audition.

The UCAS application form is, therefore, the only medium that most students can use to sell themselves. Note my use of the word 'sell'. This is deliberate. The British are often reluctant to sell themselves well; they think that it is either boasting, evidence of an over-inflated ego or worse!

This is a mistake. You need to write in a way that is persuasive, emphasises your strengths, minimises your weaknesses and essentially 'sells' you (the applicant) to the reader (the admissions tutor). The admissions tutor is the 'gatekeeper' and if your personal statement is not engaging, undersells your achievements or is poorly constructed, then the tutor will be less inclined to offer you a set of keys!

HOW DO THE UNIVERSITIES USE YOUR STATEMENT?

The University of Leicester student support service suggests on its website that your personal statement gives you the opportunity to:

- help the university find out about you and your suitability for the course they have to offer
- present your goals, experiences and qualifications in the best possible light
- demonstrate your writing ability
- distinguish yourself from the other applicants.

Note: If a candidate is unfortunate enough not to achieve the grades of the offer, often the admissions team read the statement again if they are toying with taking an applicant anyway!

THE BASICS

UK students use the UCAS online application system. You can register through your school or college. Mature students can also register as lone applicants. You enter your personal statement onto the online application.

You cannot write more than 4,000 characters (including spaces) or 47 lines of text in a standard 12 font. You cannot use italics, bold or underlined words, as these will not be transferred into the online package. Inexplicably, neither will accents such as é.

Don't waste your time on fancy formatting. The online application system will not allow indented lines or coloured fonts. It does allow all the common punctuation marks.

You should write your personal statement using Microsoft Word or an equivalent piece of software. Once it has been thoroughly checked for spelling, punctuation and grammar, you can copy and paste it into the application. If in doubt about punctuation or grammar, ask someone who knows!

In my experience, many applicants leave writing the first draft of their personal statement until the very last moment, sometimes weeks or months after they have chosen their course. Teachers are busy, too, and although sixth-form UCAS tutors are usually experienced, leaving things to the last minute can lead to errors slipping through. This is more often than not the fault of the student, so start early and keep to school or college deadlines!

WHEN TO START?

This is an easy question, as the answer is succinct – early! By that I mean during your lower sixth-form year. I ask my students to write a rough draft in the gap between the end of their lower sixth exams and the end of the summer term. This forces them to:

- make some early decisions about what to study
- look at themselves critically
- begin the research that is vital to prevent poor choices in the long term.

It means that they return in the autumn with something to go on. The autumn term is very busy and anything that puts you ahead of the game is worthwhile. This is particularly true if you need to apply early – by 15 October, 18:00 (UK time), for places at Oxford, Cambridge, medical, veterinary or dental schools.

If you want to apply for an Oxbridge choral or organ scholarship, you will need to get it done in the first week of September!

A good personal statement will probably take three weeks to write. So do not leave it till the last minute.

THE STRUCTURE OF YOUR STATEMENT

I would recommend that you divide your statement into three distinct sections.

First section: your choice of subject

This is the largest section and should be 50% of the total.

Think about the following questions and note down your answers.

- Why have you chosen to read the subject at university?
- What is the background to your interest in the subject?
- For how long have you had this interest?
- What particular areas of your studies appeal to you most and why?
- What evidence of wider reading or experience beyond the syllabus can you produce, particularly within the subjects directly relevant to your chosen subject? **This particular point is crucial and often grossly under-estimated.**

Many applicants simply do not read anything beyond their textbooks. This is not a successful way to convince an admissions tutor that you deserve to spend three more years studying them to degree level! You should name books, articles or media events that have inspired or challenged you, and be able to explain why. Listing a series of books without evaluation of at least one main theme is mere name dropping. If you are likely to be called for interview, be prepared to discuss some of the references at length. In other words – do not lie!

Mention any relevant work experience, summer employment or voluntary work that supports your application. This is vital when applying for all medical-based courses, where they will expect you to have arranged suitable work experience. For instance, you will not be interviewed for a physiotherapy course if you have not done at least two weeks' work placement.

- Have you completed any relevant taster courses in preparation for your degree course such as Headstart, Vet-Medlink or Medlink?
- Have you taken part in a NAGTY (National Academy for Gifted and Talented Youth) course?
- Have you spent any time on a residential course run by a university?

- Have you participated in any widening participation events at a local university?
- What did you learn from any of these courses?
- How useful were the courses?

These are very good selling points that you must emphasise. With all the above, tell the admissions tutor what you learnt from doing them and how they have helped you in your studies and decision making.

Second section: the subjects you are currently studying and the skills that you have learnt as a result
This should account for perhaps 30% of the total.

- What particular interests do you have within your current courses – A level or equivalent?
- How have they helped you to choose the course you are hoping to apply for?

Mention all of your subjects and briefly explain which parts of the course you have found most interesting and why. However, where a subject is directly relevant to the subject you are hoping to read, greater emphasis must be given to your enjoyment and skills in that discipline.

- What evidence of wider reading or experience beyond the syllabus can you produce, particularly within the subjects directly relevant to your chosen subject?
  This is crucial and often grossly under-estimated

Third section: your extra-curricular pursuits and skills
This is the final section and 20% of the total.

This section focuses particularly on your extra-curricular pursuits (both in and out of school or college). You can also emphasise important skills you possess, such as leadership, initiative and personal skills.

The final paragraphs should give evidence of the following areas.

- Extra-curricular subjects: what subjects are you studying outside the curriculum?
- Other achievements: these achievements should be substantive and show that you are both able and dedicated. High grades in music or drama exams, Duke of Edinburgh Awards, Combined Cadet Force (CCF) or Scout awards are all worthy examples.

- Leadership potential: give evidence of your leadership potential, how you were selected (elected?) and what you learnt from leading your team.
- Inside school: have you held positions of significant responsibility, for example head boy or girl, house captain or prefect; chair of the student council, debating society, enterprise teams, 2.0% interest rate challenge; or sports captain?
- Outside school: local political party work, charity work, church choir, uniformed organisation, young church leader, non-school sporting achievement.
- Other successes: details of significant other successes you have enjoyed – these may include community and charity work, for example, running the London Marathon, or anything else that sets you apart from the couch potatoes with their eyes glued to Sky or the latest PS4 game!
- Gap year: mention any gap year plans you have, accentuating the positive advantages of such a gap year for your future vocation. Most universities are happy to offer you a deferred place, but Oxbridge tends not to encourage deferred applications for mathematicians, and that is also true of other major universities. This is something to research and consider carefully before you fill in your UCAS form.

PLEASE NOTE

If you are applying to Oxford or Cambridge it is worth knowing that they value extra-curricular activities and work experience only if they help to demonstrate how you meet the selection criteria, as they select only on academic merit. This is certainly not the case at other universities, so do include this information but do not expect it to help your application to Oxbridge unless it meets their exacting expectations!

I have deliberately divided the statement into two large sections and one smaller section. Universities are places of academic study and research. Most admissions tutors are highly educated, committed (sometimes devoted) to their subject and keen to work with like-minded undergraduates.

They do want to recruit students with other interests, too. However, being a good rugby player, musician and pool player will not cut much ice if your academic profile is weaker than the next applicant's.

CHAPTER FIVE

HOW TO AVOID A POOR PERSONAL STATEMENT

These tips are all drawn from experience and as a result of direct advice from admissions tutors. You should read them together with the academic profiles later in Part Two of this book. They will give specific advice about different academic disciplines and are therefore well worth reading carefully.

- Clarity: Avoid waffle, generalisations and poor sentence construction. Be precise and concise. Say what you mean in a clear, uncluttered manner.
- Tone: Avoid humour – this is a professional document. Weak applicants misjudge the tone of the document they are writing.
- Style: Avoid 'text-speak', colloquial slang and language that may offend.
- Length: Use the full amount of space that you can. This is probably the most important document you have written outside of an exam hall in your life. If you cannot say enough about your passion for the subject and why you are an interesting person to teach using the full 47 lines, what does that say about you?
- Enthusiasm: Don't be dull – dry, uninspiring prose indicates a dry, uninspiring applicant. Appear very interested, enthusiastic and well read, with an informed judgement about what the course is about.
- Sell yourself: Promote your achievements and potential.
- Language: Avoid poor spelling, grammar and punctuation. This is crucial if you want to be taken seriously in any application you make, be it to university or to a job. If this is a personal weakness that you are aware of, ask someone else to proofread your statement. This is particularly relevant if you are an international student or if English is not your first language. Applications without spelling mistakes have been known to receive offers; those with mistakes may be self-penalising.
- Be yourself: Don't try to be the 'ideal' applicant. They want to get to know you, not the person you are pretending to be. After all, if you kid them into taking you, you may find when you start the course that you are not cut out for it. This is both demoralising and expensive if you subsequently leave.
- Avoid plagiarism: Do not copy anyone else's personal statement. You will read exemplary personal statements in this book, written by successful applicants. Learn

from them and the advice given by the tutors who picked them. Please do not copy them – this gives a false impression to the tutor and is fraudulent. You are asked to sign that everything in the application is correct to your knowledge. Any lies or plagiarism uncovered will be treated seriously and may jeopardise your application. Most universities now employ tools to detect plagiarism among their own students.

Below is some advice direct from the admissions departments of a variety of UK universities that mirrors and builds on the tips above.

Head of admissions for the University of Sheffield, Alan Carlisle, stresses the importance of a striking opening, but warns:

> **"** Using humour or a radical statement to get the attention of an admissions tutor can go wrong – particularly if your opening line suggests that Hitler wasn't all bad, or that the first time you were on stage was in your mother's womb. Yes, real examples … **"**

> **"** Charity work or being captain of a sports team is very positive and can be great as part of a statement – but make sure whatever you include has relevance to what you are applying for. **"**
> **ADMISSIONS TUTOR FROM THE UNIVERSITY OF SOUTHAMPTON**

The University of Manchester's head of widening participation, Julian Skyrme, encourages taking a straightforward approach:

> **"** We're asking 'why does your part-time job relate to you being an engineer?' Nail your experience to the course. Personal statements can sometimes appear like a biography. **"**

According to UCAS's own database, here are the top ten most commonly used opening sentences in UK personal statements from data published in 2013. Ones to avoid, I suggest!

Top 10 most overused personal statement opening sentences

1 I am currently studying a BTEC National Diploma in … (used 464 times)

2 From a young age I have always been interested in … (309 times)

3 From an early age I have always been interested in … (292 times)

4   Nursing is a very challenging and demanding career … (275 times)

5   For as long as I can remember I have been fascinated with … (196 times)

6   'Fashion is not something that exists in dresses only' … (189 times)

7   Nursing is a profession I have always looked upon with … (178 times)

8   For as long as I can remember I have been interested in … (166 times)

9   I am an International Academy student and have been studying since … (141 times)

10   Academically, I have always been a very determined and … (138 times)

WARNING – Don't copy a personal statement from the internet!

UCAS uses a system called 'Copycatch', which compares every application submitted with thousands posted on websites and over a million submitted in previous years. If three sentences or more – 10% of your personal statement – appear to have been copied, the form will be passed to staff for further scrutiny. Be warned! There is evidence that a significant proportion of students do lift material directly from other applicants' personal statements. Not only is this fraudulent, it is also unfair to yourself, as, in the final analysis, you want to go to a university that suits you, not the person you are trying to imitate!

Before we start to construct your personal statement, here are some final thoughts for you to consider.

MORE QUESTIONS TO ASK

These questions are more focused on the drafting stage. You will need to write your answers down so that you can look at them again, together with the other notes you have already made.

What subject/subjects do you want to study at university? List the reasons why you are drawn to this subject.	This is one of the key elements of any successful personal statement. You need to have a pithy and well-written statement of why you want to study your chosen subject, with some supporting evidence that will back up your claims.
Who or what has influenced you the most to study your subject?	For example, is there something that's triggered your interest in the subject – did you go to a lecture or have a really good teacher? Or if you've just read a book, mention that. But don't make it up. If you have not had any particular 'eureka' moment, and it is just a subject that you've loved at school, then say so.

What wider reading have you done to support this application?	Do not just mention the books you have had to read in the A level course! What magazines, newspapers and internet sites do you read or visit to extend your knowledge?
Have you attended taster courses or undertaken work experience? If appropriate, list the plays, films or TV programmes you have seen and say how they have influenced you.	This evidence should be presented clearly in the opening paragraph of your personal statement.
What research have you undertaken that has led you to this degree choice?	I just want to be sure that you have done the research necessary to make this decision. Do you know the course content well and does this meet your own skills, interests and aspirations?
What subjects have you studied so far that support this application? Do you need any particular subject at A level (or equivalent) in order to be accepted?	This is a vital part of a successful personal statement. Please do not fall into the trap of applying for a course that you cannot get into because you lack the minimum academic credentials. Many admissions tutors I spoke to complained about this weak and lazy approach that was often exposed in the personal statement.
Can you list the skills that you have developed in each course you are studying (or have studied) that support your application?	These may be analytical, mathematical, problem solving, written, oral or simply subject-specific. For instance, the study of maths may have taught you analytical skills; design, spatial awareness; or English, the ability to read and write quickly and persuasively under pressure. This is a key component of the second section of a good personal statement.
What coursework projects or extended pieces of work have you completed or been asked	Universities are keen to hear about skills that you may have already developed that are linked to university teaching and assessment styles,

to do as part of your course (if applicable)? What skills have you developed or do you expect to develop?	particularly independent learning, research and extended essays.
What are your future intentions and goals (after school and university)?	This is relevant information to include in the final paragraph. If you are unsure, do not worry, as this is nice-to-know information but by no means critical. You may want to mention any gap year plans, but only if they will enable you to be a more proficient or able student as a result. For instance, foreign travel to a country whose language you hope to study.
What extra-curricular accomplishments do you wish to draw to the attention of the admission tutors, and why?	These are important to mention in the final section of your statement. Concentrate on a few significant achievements, particularly if they involve leadership roles, personal initiative, team-building skills or the attainment of recognised qualifications.

The aim of this guide is to provide you with information that is clear, current and supported by the universities. A successful personal statement and UCAS application as a whole is one that stands out.

SUMMARY

You will now have answered many questions that are all relevant to your personal statement. You now need to look again at the notes you have made of your answers.

At this stage try to draw the notes into three groups that match the three distinct sections of the personal statement. To remind you: the first section is, broadly speaking, a clear explanation of why you want to study that course, together with evidence to support this interest. The second section is a summary of the skills and attributes that you have acquired through the study of your A levels or their equivalents, with special emphasis on the skills that are most relevant. The final section is a summary of your extra-curricular pursuits, placing particular emphasis on the activities that emphasise your leadership potential or personal initiative.

Look again at the advice given in Chapter Four for further help. Once done, you can start the first section of your personal statement.

CHAPTER SIX
THE FIRST SECTION: YOUR CHOICE OF SUBJECT

First impressions really do count. Look at the successful personal statements provided by universities later in this book. Giving your personal statement a strong opening will engage the reader's attention from the outset. Common mistakes include the use of clichéd and overused sentences in the introduction. For example, you should avoid starting your sentence with the following:

'I have always wanted to study ...'

as this is patently not the case; or

'My passion has always been for ...'

which is a similarly unlikely claim for any 18-year-old to make! You should instead imply an interest in your chosen course. You need to quickly show the admissions tutor that you have a genuine interest, and this requires the use of specific examples.

Look back at your answers to the questions in Chapter Five. What examples can you give?

Perhaps it is the books that you have read beyond the syllabus, the lecture you attended in your free time, the taster course you paid to attend in the holidays or the work experience placement you have either completed or arranged.

You could refer to a leader in the field of your interest who has inspired you – for instance, a philosophy and politics applicant could write about Plato's *Republic* and its views on the structure of democracy and justice.

You may refer directly to an event or person in your life that has inspired you – for instance, a student of mine recently wrote about her interest in medicine being linked to the fact that she has lived with a genetic disease. Her personal investigation into this illness – its aetiology and likely development – plus repeated exposure to medical professionals was the genesis of her desire to study medicine.

You will also need to draw attention to any work experience that is relevant and, most importantly, to what you learnt while undertaking this experience.

WORK EXPERIENCE

It is vital to mention relevant work experience in the opening half of the personal statement if the course requires it. Admissions tutors ask applicants to get relevant experience for two main reasons.

- **To demonstrate commitment to your career choice:** a committed applicant to medicine must demonstrate a commitment to the community, which could mean working as a hospital porter during the holidays, attending a hospice as a helper over six months, spending at least one day in a GP's surgery or taking the time to arrange a meeting with a consultant. You could work in a charity shop or with young people in a Cubs pack. One student of mine won a place after spending the summer working in an undertaker's! Be creative!
- **So that they can be sure you are going into this career path with your eyes open:** you've seen the reality of the job, warts and all, and it hasn't put you off. A potential applicant to teacher training needs to be aware that pupils are not always well behaved and that teaching involves a great deal of time-consuming administration. They learn this by sitting in with a primary class and talking to teachers at their local senior school. In my experience, schools are nearly always willing to offer a potential undergraduate the opportunity to do this if they write well in advance.

The most common courses that expect work experience are:

Medicine: The medical school at the University of Sheffield has the following advice for potential applicants.

> A good personal statement will include information on your relevant work experience. Medical schools expect applicants to have a range of work experience for two reasons. Firstly, this demonstrates that you have a realistic insight to the profession – you are, after all, committing to a lifetime career when you apply to study medicine. It is important that you have

an understanding of the complex nature of a doctor's role, as well as being aware of the highs and lows of the profession.

> Work experience is also important in enabling you to develop (and to demonstrate that you have) the relevant skills and qualities that are essential to becoming a good doctor. A few examples are listed below.

- Communication skills
- A sense of service to the community
- A sense of responsibility
- Self-insight
- Energy
- Enthusiasm
- Perseverance
- Ability to overcome setbacks
- Ability to work independently
- Experience of working with diverse groups.

> We recognise that it is not always possible for students to obtain work placements in a medical environment, given the limited availability of volunteer placements in hospitals and similar clinical settings now. However, there are many areas related to medicine in which you can gain experience. Some examples of these are listed below.

- Paid or voluntary work experience in a residential care home, hospice or similar.
- Working in a youth centre or working with young children.
- Participating in community volunteering schemes.
- Shadowing a GP or other medical practitioner to gain an insight to their role, responsibilities and the complexities of healthcare.
- Working with a diverse range of people (whether on a paid or voluntary basis).

> **"** Participatory work experience (not simply observing, but a 'hands on' role) is extremely valuable. Many applicants arrange to undertake paid or voluntary work as a Healthcare Assistant. Whatever work experience you have, it is important that you reflect effectively on this in your personal statement. **"**

Most medical schools expect at least two discrete work experience placements. Many hospitals now do not offer ward-based work experience to those under 18. Try your local hospital's human resources department, but do not be surprised by a refusal. You are also quite likely to be able to arrange a visit to your local GP to have lunch with a doctor to discuss his or her career and recent issues in the NHS that may come up in an interview. A well-crafted letter to your own GP can pay dividends. Mentoring younger pupils in your own school can help your interpersonal skills, and work with disabled teenagers promotes empathy.

Dentistry: My experience is that dental surgeries are generally happy to have a well-chosen potential dentist in their surgery for a few days. Write in the first instance to the practice manager. Always give a reference from your school, as they will probably want to check you out with a teacher at the school first.

Two recent students of mine did that and made such a good impression that the dentist sent the university a recommendation letter with their application. Priceless! They are now both doing dentistry at university, and neither is the son or daughter of a dentist or medic.

Nursing and midwifery: Queen Mary University of London (QMUL) suggests that care homes and hospices are excellent settings in which students can find out if they are really suited to this type of work. For midwifery, applicants should contact their local hospital's midwifery service manager to arrange experience in the maternity unit – most universities will require a minimum of one day's experience, if nothing else, so that students can learn that being a midwife is not about babies! It's actually about looking after the mothers.

Physiotherapy: Similarly, the QMUL website says that physiotherapy is probably one of the most competitive courses a student can apply for, so getting work experience is essential. Most jobs are in the NHS, so experience in this setting should be the student's main priority, even if they are aiming to work in sport (a growing, but still very small, area of physiotherapy work). It is sometimes possible to get a paid (rarely) or voluntary physiotherapy assistant post in an NHS hospital; failing that, shadowing a chartered physiotherapist is the next best thing.

Veterinary science: There are only six veterinary schools in the UK and competition to get in is fierce, although the myth that you need all A*s at GCSE needs exploding! Potential applicants need to spend time with both small and large animals, and this may be problematic if you live in an urban environment. Another important point, according to a source in the Royal Veterinary College, is that they are now looking actively to recruit *male* applicants. Too many girls are applying, apparently!

However, most veterinary surgeries are used to written requests for help, so start there. Think laterally – you may live near a children's farm; they look after animals and you could volunteer to work there. One successful student that I knew did this at a local children's farm from the age of 14. She is now a successful vet in London. If you own a pony or horse, the stables will have qualified professionals on hand to advise. Most stables will be delighted to offer you unpaid experience working with their animals.

Note: all of the above will expect you to undertake an enhanced disclosure test or Disclosure and Barring Service (DBS) check and, in the case of medicine, to be inoculated against certain diseases (especially Hepatitis B) before you start the course.

Here are some examples of excellent opening paragraphs from real personal statements that were all successful in gaining offers at Oxford, Cambridge or other leading universities.

THE ARCHAEOLOGY AND ANTHROPOLOGY APPLICANT

Having spent the first 13 years of my life in Kenya, it was always going to be a culture shock when I moved to England four years ago. My time in both countries has given me a better perspective on the globe on which we live. From a young age I was fascinated by the human race. Through visits to Samburu and Maasai settlements and day-to-day living in Nairobi, I began to realise the great diversity within human culture, further revealed by trips to Kenya's Islamic coast and then by a move to England. Here I experienced a very different outlook and a very different way of life, captured well in 'Watching the English' by Kate Fox. My own life has triggered a need to understand more about the reasons for these differences. I hunger to learn about 'the self' while studying 'the other', to know who we are and how we got where we are. Anthropology is the obvious route to this knowledge.

THE CLASSICS APPLICANT

Classics is for me both fascinating and mind-stretching. I view its insistence on total understanding of complex grammar, creative literary criticism, stringent philosophical analysis, and various other disciplines, as an essential beginning of what I hope to carve into a scholar's life. My first encounter with Greek tragedy lay with a verse translation of 'The Oresteian Trilogy' whose formal structure, elegant language and emotional intensity struck me deeply. I was amazed to find myself laying aside all my atheistic ideals, instead fearing the wrath of ancient deities. Sophocles similarly forced me to care about King Oedipus; the end to the plot, known to the audience, the reader and Tiresias, made further reading an unpleasant prospect, whilst the righteousness of Oedipus' struggle to help his own people made me continue out of hope for a different fate. I was thus compelled to witness human suffering from the reflectively remote yet intimately shocking perspective of the theatre and truly learnt the meaning of catharsis from those four plays.

THE ENGLISH APPLICANT

The study of English literature has undoubtedly shaped the way I think. Philosophical deliberation has been a necessity in the reading of both 'Paradise Lost' and 'Hamlet', for example, with Milton's attempts to 'justify the ways of God to men' being pertinent to Hamlet's lamentation of the human condition and what he perceives to be the sheer inevitability of suffering through life. The exploration of the historical contexts behind these two works has been equally absorbing, with the similarities between the God of Paradise Lost, and the king condemned by Milton, lending a particularly revealing insight to Milton's own disposition. Indeed, through learning English, I have encountered a wide range of disciplines, and it is the extreme diversity offered by the subject that makes it so wonderful and informative for me; rigorous analytical thought is developed through practical criticism, while the flexibility and creativity of writing is cultivated through essay and prose composition.

THE MATHEMATICS AND ACTUARIAL SCIENCE APPLICANT

Mathematics is not just a mere subject but a universal language. Its plethora of Greek symbols interlaced with numbers makes it seem like a clandestine code, which has to be deciphered. This aside, I believe the real magic of mathematics lies not with its method of execution, but its definite solutions founded on irrefutable proofs, not ignoring the seemingly endless array of applications. Having studied physics, my awareness of these applications has increased substantially. For instance, the laws laid down by Newtonian mechanics are seen to govern the everyday world and are difficult not to witness. In computing, I have explored the logical arm of mathematics put into practice: finite state machines, Boolean equations and the programming languages themselves. Even chemistry, like my other subjects, echoes the hallmarks of maths. Through reading Du Sautoy's 'Finding Moonshine' I discovered that chemistry, the study of molecular interaction, utilises mathematics in the form of symmetry. Overall, it never ceases to amaze me how mathematics seems to be everywhere at once, even in places you expect not to find it.

THE HISTORY APPLICANT

Growing up in London, I have been exposed to the city's history from a very young age. While appreciating the myriad historical eras that have shaped the development of London, it is the Victorian era that fascinates me the most. Throughout this period of significant change, from the Industrial Revolution to the suffrage movement, London has incessantly remained at the centre of history. Recently I have developed a particular interest in how changes, such as the decline of the Liberal party and the rise of the Labour party, have deeply rooted themselves in our society, and continue to be felt in our political system today. In this way history has shaped contemporary life and continues to mould, influence and develop it. My affinity with the Victorians reached its fullest this year when I studied 19th and early 20th century British politics. As such, the study of history has opened up my eyes to the textures and contours of society as we see it today, allowing me a greater understanding of contemporary issues.

THE MEDICAL APPLICANT

The aim of every branch of medicine is to alleviate avoidable suffering in the human body and mind. Caring for a person's needs by providing a cure, managing a condition or maintaining general health is a role that I look forward to, for its intellectual stimulation and emotional fulfilment. Medicine is not stagnant; developments in patient care, technology and new treatments will leave me constantly challenged and needing to update my knowledge and skills. I hope to be able to contribute to the body of research, hopefully into infectious diseases in the developing world and gynaecology, two areas of particular interest to me. I am drawn to medicine by my analytical and inquisitive mind, as a profession that presents questions answered using a range of tools as well as innovative thinking.

A SOCIAL WORK APPLICANT

I am applying for a place to study social work because I have always wanted to be able to make a difference to people's lives. With social work I believe I can do this in a caring and supportive way. I have gained some insight into mental health while caring for my grandma and the difficulties she faced on a daily basis while suffering with Alzheimer's disease. This is one area I would like to gain more knowledge of. Another family member suffered from drug and alcohol addiction, and I witnessed the effects it had on his mental health and the effects drugs had on his family. These personal experiences instilled in me further the desire to become a social worker.

SUMMARY

Draft this first section carefully, using a word processor. Make sure that you ask advice from a teacher or tutor and that it is read by at least two people who can check it for quality and possible error. Do not worry too much at this stage about length. It is easier to précis a long, well-written piece than to pad it out. You will in the end need to cut it down to meet the length requirements, but this can wait until later.

CHAPTER SEVEN

THE SECOND SECTION: THE SUBJECTS YOU ARE CURRENTLY STUDYING

 our personal statement must proceed in a logical succession from one thought to the next. The body of your personal statement should lead in a convincing way from the introduction to the conclusion.

The second section should focus on the skills you have already gained while at school or college. When talking about your educational background, do not just mention what is clear from the rest of your application. The admissions tutors can read elsewhere how many GCSEs you got.

The primary focus should be on any A level courses that are directly relevant to your choice of degree. The historian should talk about his or her history A level first and at greatest length. Focus on what you have learnt and what skills you have honed.

When you introduce your other AS or A level subjects, it is wise to draw attention to the ways in which your other subjects have complemented your skills and learning in the principal subject.

- Talk first and foremost about the subjects that you are currently or have recently finished studying that are directly relevant to your choice of degree. How have they helped you choose the course?
- Do not repeat what an admissions tutor can read elsewhere – telling them how many GCSEs you have got is irrelevant.
- Do mention, however, if you have any very high marks in AS or GCSE papers – this sets you apart from the rest. By this I mean that you may have obtained 100% in one paper or full marks in your extended or project work.
- Mention any coursework or extended project that you have completed that suggests that you are capable of independent learning. This is an important facet of university teaching and learning.
- Mention the other subjects that may not be directly relevant, but have enabled you to gain useful skills.

- Mention any books, magazines, websites or courses that you may have read or attended. However, do not lie, as this can be exposed at a later date and lead to rejection.

Good examples of the above can be found in these extracts from real personal statements.

THE CHEMISTRY APPLICANT

Currently I am reading 'Why Chemical Reactions Happen' by James Keeler and Peter Wothers, which is challenging my understanding of what I have learnt and taking me beyond the boundaries of the A level course into wave function and the associated quantum mechanics. Although the material is at a higher level than my current studies I can use my knowledge and understanding from the work I have done so far to get to grips with more complex ideas. It has taught me to think objectively and formulate my own ideas from the information provided. Alongside chemistry I study medieval history and biology and have already gained an A in A level Mathematics. Although chemistry is by far my favourite subject I also have a compelling curiosity about other areas of science, some of which biology has helped to satisfy. Studying human biology, in particular learning about how our bodies work, is fascinating, although I enjoy biology most when we study processes that involve using chemical knowledge, such as respiration. Over the years I have won four prizes in science, including ones for chemistry and biology this year. Medieval history has been valuable as there is no text book, so a lot of research must be undertaken outside of class, using contemporary and modern sources. This independent learning is crucial in allowing me to develop skills that will aid me when studying at degree level.

THE MATHEMATICS APPLICANT

As part of my A level Mathematics coursework I chose to use computer programs to develop various numerical solutions to equations. I enjoyed using software such as Excel and an online graph plotter. This led me to begin to appreciate how computers can help deepen one's understanding of mathematics as well as being a useful problem-solving tool. I think delving more deeply into the studies of computers will enable me to apply mathematics in a wider range of situations, such as in physics and modelling in economics. Due to family circumstances I spent a year studying in Hong Kong, where I took an accounting course which I greatly enjoyed, and it gave me some ideas about what is involved in a career in accountancy. Mathematics plays an important role in accounting: first, in making the necessary calculations and, then, in interpreting the financial data. Accounting has sparked a general interest in business. I enjoy analysing how the firms put all the input factors together to produce goods at the lowest cost and highest margins. Studying AS Economics also made me realise the complexity of the global economy. The large amount of graphical interpretation and data interpolation has allowed me to understand the essential importance of having fundamental mathematical skills.

THE ECONOMICS APPLICANT

I chose to study maths as I enjoy how it conveys logic in numbers and variables; it has improved my analytical skills. I regularly compete in the Maths Challenge. I feel maths will definitely be of an advantage during my years in university and when I, hopefully, enter a career within the field of economics. English language has taught me the ability to tailor written work directed at a particular audience using an appropriate format. Biology and chemistry have allowed me to refine my skills in drawing results from scientific evidence. They have also taught me the importance of precision and attention to detail. These skills can be extended to assessing and evaluating data in the economy.

THE MODERN LANGUAGES APPLICANT

While at school I have gained eight academic prizes, including three for French and two for Latin. My study of Latin has been particularly useful for setting up a framework within which to learn languages, as well as for its rich history and literature. In English, I have nurtured a love for literature and developed analytical and evaluative skills. Studying history at AS helped me come to a greater understanding of the foundations of our European culture, as well as similarly furthering analytical and evaluative techniques.

THE AMERICAN STUDIES APPLICANT

In GCSE History, I was intrigued with our topics on the Gold Rush, the first cowboys, outlaws, vigilantes and the manipulation of the Native Americans which led to their ultimate demise. In English, we are reading 'The Handmaid's Tale' by Margaret Atwood, learning her views on the oppression of women within modern society. Doing further research on dictatorships and the dominance of power, such as in the USA, has fascinated me greatly. Reading 'The Big Sleep' by Raymond Chandler last year was exciting due to the links with 1930s prohibition America and the corrupt police force; all dramatised as a novel. Studying it allowed me to formulate my opinions about the novel into an analytical argument under a strict deadline.

CHAPTER EIGHT

THE THIRD SECTION: YOUR EXTRA-CURRICULAR INTERESTS AND ACHIEVEMENTS

This is the final paragraph and should focus on your extra-curricular pursuits. Although your academic potential is top of their minds, admissions tutors do want to recruit students who will bring other skills to the department and university as a whole. They are looking for someone who is academically motivated but not a couch potato.

You need in this section to attempt to show some distinct skills or personality traits. The key skills that admissions tutors tell us they look for are:

- persistence
- independence
- self-motivation
- leadership
- maturity.

Think now about what you do outside the classroom. What are your primary extra-curricular pursuits? How have these pursuits helped you to develop the skills that admissions tutors are looking for?

Add a concluding sentence or two. This will tie everything together. Integrate all the information gathered in the above paragraphs and finish on two positive sentences. The closing sentence must be powerful and succinct.

- Emphasise personal attributes that might include organisational skills, punctuality, sensitivity, responsibility, initiative, efficiency, communication and empathy. Where you mention one of these, give an example of what you have done to expose and develop this attribute.
- Mention any subjects that you are studying outside the formal curriculum, particularly if they are academic in their focus or lead to nationally recognised qualifications.

- Mention the extra-curricular activities that you have undertaken. Don't just write a list. Concentrate on two or three activities that emphasise your personal qualities, such as leadership skills, initiative, sporting success or debating skills. The Duke of Edinburgh's Award, Young Enterprise Scheme and Combined Cadet Force (CCF) or Scouts are all particularly good examples.

- Emphasise any roles that you have held that were significant – particularly if you were elected, or appointed by a senior teacher. For example, prefect status, captaincy of a sports team or elected head of an activity.

- Mention career plans or gap year plans – make sure that your gap year plans accentuate the positive advantages of such a gap year for your future vocation or university career.

- As I indicated earlier in the book, Oxford and Cambridge are not going to consider relevant any work experience or extra-curricular skills you have that do not have a bearing on your academic application. This is unique to them, but worth bearing in mind.

Another popular ending is one where you opt for a little self-promotion: 'Overall I believe I have the necessary (academic/intellectual) ability, motivation and stamina to cope successfully with the demands of this subject and look forward to hearing from you in due course.'

Here are some examples of extracts from good final paragraphs that proved to be successful.

THE ENGLISH APPLICANT

I greatly enjoy playing sport, and have represented the school for the past two years in the football and tennis 1st XIs, and the rugby 2nd XV. In 2007 I spent two weeks helping at Bushfire Orphanage in Uganda, an experience I found both challenging and greatly enjoyable. I am also greatly interested in writing, and have proofread novels for Caroline Lawrence (a children's author), as well as proofreading a script for Bradley Quirk, a proofreader at the UK Film Council.

THE GEOGRAPHY APPLICANT

Travel constitutes for me a real excitement, whether through school trips to the volcanoes and glaciers of Iceland and the eroded coast of Malta with its hugely exciting opportunities for scuba diving, or on journeys with the National Children's Orchestra to the Czech Republic and the County Youth Orchestra to Cyprus. Such travel has given me much food for thought on both economic and physical issues that impinge on globalisation. I have recently accepted an invitation to travel to Australia as a gap year student, mainly to teach hockey and other sports, an opportunity that would not only enhance my knowledge of geography, but also improve my leadership skills.

THE ENGINEERING APPLICANT

My main hobby is mountain biking and I have been riding regularly for 4 years. During this time, I have had to carry out a lot of maintenance on my bike, which has led to my interest in how they work and all the aspects of bike development. For example, carbon fibre is replacing aluminum as the material of choice for most components due to its ability to improve strength while reducing weight. This interest has led me to taking a course on advanced mountain bike maintenance in November. I have taken part in many activities that have helped to build my teamwork, leadership and time management skills. I finished the Duke of Edinburgh Bronze Award where strong teamwork is essential in order to succeed, especially at the expedition. I have also represented my year on the school council, where I had to demonstrate good time management and organisational skills, which I used when I helped to organise an event to help other schools improve their councils. I have played cricket for my school and local team, which has taught me to cope well with pressure.

THE MEDICAL APPLICANT

My extra-curricular commitments are significant and include representing the school at the highest level in football and rugby, serving as House Captain and now school prefect, which not only involves working as part of a team but carries with it responsibility for others and leadership, offering younger students peer support. These skills came together when I volunteered at an old People's Care Home project, opening my eyes to the needs of the elderly in our community. I believe I excel at this because I am a non-judgemental person who empathises with others and understands the importance of having someone to listen to them. I am committed to a long-term career in medicine and am well aware of the unique demands of the role.

THE NATURAL SCIENCE APPLICANT

outside the classroom, I am in the 1st XV for rugby, and we recently went to Australia on tour and won all six matches. My passionate and driven nature allowed me to raise the funds to take my place on the tour. I am also undertaking my Duke of Edinburgh Gold Award after having completed bronze and silver. I also enjoy taking to the stage from time to time, and played Bottom in the school's production of 'A Midsummer Night's Dream'. At university I plan to work to achieve my employment potential and expand my love and knowledge of chemistry. I have a strong desire to go into research chemistry and develop new compounds; most likely drug discovery or maybe even research into new materials. The reason I am so enthralled with the research aspect of chemistry is because I know that there are endless possibilities for discovery of new and useful compounds due to the advances already made by humans. Being a part of this scientific advance would be a privilege and honour that I am wholeheartedly willing to work for.

CHAPTER NINE
THE FINAL POLISH

 great personal statement is a work of art, not a hastily written paragraph or two. It takes time to research, plan, draft and then re-draft. Do not be afraid to re-draft many times.

Use the three drafts that you have begun and, if you have not already done so, word process your handwritten thoughts and begin the final drafting process.

You can enter between 1,000 and 4,000 characters or a maximum of 47 lines of text (including spaces and blank lines) for your personal statement.

You need to consider the following when you redraft.

- **SPAG (Spelling, Punctuation and Grammar):** do not be guilty of poor SPAG. If you are, the impression you give will be poor. As I intimated earlier, ask someone who is a competent proofreader to check this carefully.
- **Present yourself in the best possible light:** make sure that your statement presents your goals, experiences and qualifications in the best possible light, as well as demonstrating your writing ability. Have you mentioned the books you have read beyond the demands of the syllabus? Have you presented your work experience in the best possible light?
- **Get rid of any repetition or wasted words:** do not say what is already apparent elsewhere in the application.
- **Avoid waffle, generalisations and poor sentence construction:** be precise and concise. Say what you mean in a clear, uncluttered manner.
- **Avoid passive writing:** rewrite sentences that use the phrase 'has been' or 'was'. These are words that are good to cull if you need to précis something that is too long.
- **Avoid the word 'I' as far as possible:** save 'I' for when you need to write a short sentence that is full of emphasis', such as 'I am a hard-working, conscientious and ambitious student'.

- **Length:** most of my students find the hardest part of the personal statement-writing process lies in the careful précising that is necessary when it is 50 characters too long. This is a skill that requires time and effort. If you are really struggling, ask for advice from a teacher or fellow student whom you know to be a good writer.
- **Be yourself, not the 'ideal' applicant:** the admissions tutors want to get to know you, not the person you are pretending to be. You will spend three years studying your chosen subject. Be sure that it is what you want, that you sell yourself well but fairly, so that when you pass the exams in August and win that place you know that it is the right place for you.

Good luck!

CHAPTER TEN
HOW TO APPLY TO MUSIC CONSERVATOIRES

You can apply to study at a music conservatoire using the UCAS Apply system. In 2015, the CUKAS system was replaced by a new UCAS process called UCAS Conservatoires. Most conservatoires offer music, but many also offer courses in drama and other performing arts. The emphasis here is on performance. Unlike degree courses, the academic element is reduced and the applicant will be expected to show a high level of performance potential, normally via audition.

You can only apply once in a cycle and the process is not that dissimilar to the process used by other undergraduate applicants.

Note: Not all UK conservatoires use the UCAS process. Some have their own application form. Currently, the Guildhall School of Music and Drama (www.gsmd.ac.uk) does not use the system and has its own application form and audition process. Please contact this school direct to obtain the latest prospectus or complete the online application form.

Here is the current list of conservatoires that use the UCAS online application:

- Birmingham Conservatoire
- Leeds College of Music
- The Royal Academy of Music
- The Royal College of Music
- The Royal Conservatoire of Scotland
- The Royal Northern College of Music
- The Royal Welsh College of Music & Drama
- Trinity Laban Conservatoire of Music & Dance.

The UCAS Conservatoires website, and links to all of the above colleges, can be found at www.ucas.com/ucas/conservatoires/getting-started/whats-different-about-conservatoire. The website has comprehensive advice about completing the application. What follows is a summary of the main points, but you are advised to read the website carefully before starting an application.

This chapter will provide you with a sound understanding of why students apply to a conservatoire, how to apply online (including what to include in the personal statement) and what to expect at audition.

WHY STUDY AT A CONSERVATOIRE?

Conservatoire education is suitable for any talented musician who is particularly interested in performance, conducting or composition. They teach to a professional standard, combining practical and academic study in an environment that is steeped in musical history. Many of the teachers are leaders in their field, and the UK is fortunate to have some of the finest conservatoires in Europe. Study in a conservatoire environment enables excellent networking and developmental opportunities for all musicians, regardless of their specialism or musical direction.

Conservatoire students have the opportunity to conduct, perform or have their music performed on numerous occasions. Many of the performances are public, and the students often find it is possible to earn money while at college by playing at private parties and other functions. The range of music teaching available is vast, including jazz, orchestral, operatic, musical theatre and choral.

Students study for three- or four-year undergraduate degrees (BA and BMus) as well as in postgraduate programmes such as MMus and PgDip.

SHOULD I GO TO AN OPEN DAY?

Absolutely. This is a very important decision and all the conservatoires have open days advertised online. This is a very useful part of the application process and will help you narrow down your options.

WHAT ARE THE ENTRY STANDARDS?

As you can imagine, competition for places is high. Your traditional academic standards play 'second fiddle' to your performance standard. Each conservatoire has its own academic and performance demands. However, I will use information provided by the Royal College of Music (RCM) to provide you with an idea of the demands likely to be placed on you and any other applicant. Most of this information is pertinent to all applicants but you are advised to look carefully at the prospectuses of the conservatoires.

The RCM currently has the following minimum entry requirements for the BMus (Hon).

■ Two A levels at grade E or above. They recommend but do not require you to take A level Music. Most applicants obtain an A or B in A level Music.

If you are not taking A level Music, but still wish to apply to the RCM, you may still be considered if you can demonstrate an appropriate level of musical knowledge and literacy. You may be tested/interviewed at audition to ascertain this.

Alternative entrance qualifications that are accepted instead of A levels are:

■ three Scottish Certificate of Education (SCE) Higher Grade passes, a grade D or above
■ two Pre-U subject passes at P3 or above
■ BTEC qualifications – NQF Level 3
■ International Baccalaureate (at least 24 points)
■ Welsh Baccalaureate (accepted as equivalent to one A level).

WHAT ABOUT AUDITIONS?

The RCM has the following audition format:

■ auditions/interviews at the RCM are approximately 15–20 minutes long
■ for some instruments and for voice you may be asked to perform at a second audition on the same day
■ for set pieces see the Audition Pieces section of the online prospectus – www.rcm.ac.uk/apply/auditions/auditionpieces
■ technical work (for example, scales and arpeggios) may be required of some instrumentalists
■ sight reading may be required of all performers
■ an accompanist can be provided by the RCM if required, but you are strongly advised to bring your own accompanist, with whom you will have worked in preparation for the audition.

Please note, each institution has its own audition procedure. Please research this information carefully before proceeding.

WHEN CAN I APPLY?

You can start an application in the July prior to attending the college in the following year. Your application deadline is normally the 1 October, 18:00 (UK time), for music courses starting in the following year and 15 January, 18:00 (UK time), for undergraduate drama, dance or screen production courses starting in the year that you intend to join.

If you miss this deadline, all is not lost. However, you will need to ask the conservatoire *before* applying if they are still taking applications.

HOW MANY CONSERVATOIRES CAN I APPLY TO?

Up to six in one application cycle.

WHAT COSTS ARE INVOLVED?

The cost of the application is similar to UCAS. In addition, you may be asked to pay audition fees. These vary from institution to institution.

CAN I APPLY TO UCAS CONSERVATOIRES AND UCAS IN THE SAME YEAR?

Yes. Indeed, you are encouraged to do so, as competition is so fierce that you need other options to fall back on. You can apply to read music at university but there is nothing stopping you applying for something entirely different and then making up your mind at a later date. Keep your options open!

CAN I APPLY FOR STUDENT FINANCE?

Of course, the same rules apply to you as to other UCAS applicants.

For more information, look at the Student Finance website: www.ucas.com/ucas/conservatoires/finance-and-support.

WHAT SHOULD I INCLUDE IN A PERSONAL STATEMENT?

The advice is broadly similar to that for UCAS personal statements, except that conservatoires are far more interested in your musical skills. You need to emphasise why you have chosen the courses you have listed. Unlike for UCAS applications, each conservatoire will know where else you have applied to. Bear this in mind. You should mention:

- why are you applying – what are your ambitions and what drives your interest
- what makes you suitable – membership of national/international orchestras, choirs or chamber groups (such as NYO, EUYO or National Youth Theatre), and any other relevant skills and achievements gained from education, work or other activities
- your experience in composition and conducting
- the music and composers that have inspired you so far
- any masterclasses you have attended, whether you have been involved in junior training programmes and any other gifted-and-talented initiatives
- what your career plans are, post-application (if known)

- any non-accredited skills and achievements that you have gained through such activities as Duke of Edinburgh Award, Young Enterprise or ASDAN (Award Scheme Development and Accreditation Network awards)
- your sports, social or leisure interests
- your gap year plans, if appropriate. You can apply for a deferred place.

As with all personal statements, heed the following basic advice.

- Always start by reading any advice that you get online from your chosen conservatoire. They will often have tips that will help you.
- Make sure that the course you are applying to meets with your skill base.
- Make your interest in the subject evident in the opening few paragraphs with clear evidence supporting this from your study so far. You are writing for a tutor who shares this passion and wants to teach students who have a genuine love for the subject. This may not always be possible, but whether it is or not, it is vital that the reader believes that you have thought about this application carefully and will thrive at that institution and department.
- Avoid spelling, punctuation and grammar errors. Get your statement proofread by someone who is competent to do so.
- Take advice where possible from a teacher who knows about the subject that you are hoping to apply for. Your teacher will be asked for a reference that testifies to your ability as a musician, actor, etc.
- Avoid plagiarism or lies.
- Write about your current skills and attributes, both academic and non-academic, in a positive and emphatic manner.
- Treat your personal statement as a very important piece of prose that deserves your best efforts. Take your time to get it right, and when it is, be proud of it and ready to defend what it says if you are called to interview.
- Ensure that you use all 4,000 characters (or near as possible).

HOW TO FILL IN THE APPLICATION FORM

The form is completed online and in many ways it resembles the UCAS Apply system. The website provides comprehensive advice and you should refer to this for details. Procedures change more often than books do, so go there for the latest information.

WHAT HAPPENS AFTER I APPLY?

- You will receive a welcome email from UCAS confirming that your application has been received.
- Your application will be read by each of your chosen conservatoires.

- There may be a wait – be patient and do not call the conservatoires unless you have still not heard anything a month after application. Many will send you an email telling you that you are being considered.
- If you pass the first hurdle, you may be called for an audition. This audition will depend on the institution and you *must* read about their audition expectations before you apply. They will not pay for your travel costs to and from the audition and a fee may have to be paid to attend the audition itself.
- Keep an eye on the progress of the application using the online Tracking service. Details are sent to you early in the application cycle.
- When you have received all your offers and rejections, you may make a final choice. You may receive an unconditional offer or a conditional offer. Full details of this process can be found on the UCAS Conservatoire website.

CHAPTER ELEVEN

ANSWERS TO FREQUENTLY ASKED QUESTIONS

Throughout the last ten years I have been asked hundreds of questions about how to prepare a winning UCAS application. This short chapter will attempt to offer answers to many of the most common questions. All my answers have been reviewed to ensure that the information is accurate and relevant for this new edition. Remember, this is my opinion and may differ from those of others, so take my advice with that in mind.

Many of the questions relate to filling in the form, so you might want to read this while completing an application online through UCAS Apply. Others are more general, but still relevant to the needs of most applicants. Good schools will provide their own guidance, and some schools have different ways of approaching things. Do ensure that you take advice from them too.

APPLYING TO UNIVERSITY

What are the best universities?
In short, the best university is the one that suits **you** the best!

It is the university that offers YOU

- a course that is interesting and meets your academic needs
- a good quality of teaching
- the right geographical location
- an offer that you are realistically going to achieve
- a good employment record for recent graduates
- good facilities.

Take the time to make up your mind and make sure the information you base your decision on is relevant, accurate and preferably based on a visit to the university. Have a look at Part Three to find more places you can turn to for guidance.

Should I go on visits and open days?

You should not commit yourself to three or more years at a university without having a good look at it and making sure you will feel comfortable there. One way of doing this is to take a trip during school holidays and to see as many places as possible.

Universities and colleges also have official open days. These can be a mixed blessing: thousands of school pupils milling around and all kinds of shows to try to capture their interest. However, if you go with clear aims and questions in mind you can learn a great deal.

Attending faraway open days, and interviews too, can be horribly expensive. You should think carefully about exactly how many universities you need to visit. All university and college open days are listed on the individual universities' websites. Apart from the cost of travelling to open days, there is also the fact that you will miss valuable teaching time in school.

What is the UCAS Tariff?

The UCAS Tariff was introduced some time ago by UCAS to assist institutions that wanted to offer Tariff rather than grade offers. For courses starting from September 2017, the Tariff will change to reflect changes in the AS and A levels. AS is now decoupled and a stand-alone qualification that has a 40%, not 50%, weighting. Not all universities use the Tariff, so look at this when you apply.

The Tariff is too big and complex to publish here, so I suggest that you look at the UCAS website (www.ucas.com) for an accurate picture.

Should I apply to Oxford or Cambridge?

Competition to gain admission to Oxford and Cambridge may be fierce in terms of academic requirements but there are fewer applicants per place than for many other universities. In the arts, around 26% to 28% of applicants will be successful in getting a place, and in the sciences the figures are 28% to 30%. A growing number of qualified candidates from throughout the world compete for the places and this, in part, ensures that a high level of academic attainment must be reached for entry. It is no longer the case that those with less strong academic grades can compensate by being more rounded individuals through excelling in activities outside the classroom. Academic ability is paramount.

It is essential, therefore, that only pupils with the strongest academic qualifications should consider making an application to Oxford or Cambridge. It is fair to say that only the top students in most schools or colleges meet their exacting standards. They both have a strong widening participation programme, with many schemes on offer to provide incentives for students from qualifying backgrounds. In these cases, entry criteria may be relaxed. The

Sutton Trust does a lot of work in this area and I recommend that you access its website (www.suttontrust.com) and look carefully at the outreach each college offers.

For most, however, a string of GCSE As and A*s and three A level grade A predictions are regarded by Oxford and Cambridge as the *minimum* requirements for consideration rather than as guarantees of admission. They do accept people with other qualifications and their websites make each Tariff clear. The successful candidates, from among hundreds of applicants who meet these threshold requirements, are those who demonstrate a knowledge and interest in their chosen subject which far exceeds the normal requirements of their AS or A2 syllabus.

The A* is now a standard offer at Cambridge; in addition, new common-format written assessments are being introduced from 2017 entry, to be taken by applicants either pre-interview or at interview. The Cambridge written assessments will be set for all subjects except mathematics and music, where applicants will be tested through short tasks at interview. Oxford is starting to make some A* offers but increasingly relies on its own pre-interview tests. Information about the range of tests expected for each subject can be found on the Oxford and Cambridge admissions pages. Take care to read up on this and think about how you might be able to prepare for such tests.

Only those applicants who in their own time and on their own initiative have completed reading and research in addition to that required by their teachers have any realistic chance of admission. The universities establish this initially from the personal statement, and it is tested in the selection process at the universities (see Chapter Seven).

However, at the same time that these universities are attempting to cultivate an intellectual and academic elite, they are also making every effort to extend access to young people from all economic and social backgrounds. Their focus on encouraging state school pupils to apply has now led to the charge that there is bias against pupils from public schools. Oxford and Cambridge are adamant that this is not the case and statistics show that student numbers from the state and independent sectors are approximately equal.

Nevertheless, in order to encourage state school pupils, both universities offer non-repayable bursaries for full-time UK and EU students with qualifying household incomes. Again, for the latest information look at the universities' websites.

The application process to Oxbridge is stressful, time consuming and labour intensive. I encourage only candidates of the highest intellectual calibre to apply. Unrealistic applications lead only to inevitable rejection and disappointment. Often, application to Oxbridge is driven by the pupils' parents, particularly in the independent sector. Teachers know the pupils and it is they, in discussion with the pupils, who should make the assessment of whether the pupil is suitable for Oxbridge. Those pupils who are interested in applying but whose academic qualifications are weaker than Oxbridge expect might be better served by applying *after* their A levels. At that point their final A2 grades will be known, resolving any questions as to their academic fitness to go to Oxbridge. Furthermore, the added year's maturity may also enhance their application. In my experience, the success rate post-A level is considerably higher than pre-A level.

Please note that applications for choral or music scholarships are equally competitive and the same academic standards are applied to those candidates.

COMPLETING THE REST OF THE UCAS FORM

When and how do I start to fill in the UCAS form?
You can start the application process from 1 September of Year 13 or in the year prior to when you hope to commence the course. This also applies if you intend to defer entry.

You can access UCAS Apply from any computer that has internet access, via www.ucas.com. If you are an applicant applying from a school or college, you will need to find out your unique buzzword. This will allow your application to be linked with others from the same institution. If you are a private applicant, not attached to a college/school, then this does not apply.

Do I need to complete my application all at once?
No, indeed this is one great advantage of UCAS Apply. Not only can you access it worldwide, but you can also save it and return to it until you are ready to 'send it to the referee'. Make sure, however, that you do save before you logout.

What is a 'buzzword'?
This is a unique word used by each UCAS registered centre. You need it to begin your application. Ask the relevant tutor for details.

What if I forget my password?
Try not to! Keep it safe, in several places, when you first register. However, if you do forget it you can often have it changed by the member of staff who is the UCAS super-user at your school or college. If not, use the 'forgotten log in' tab to reset your password.

What address should I use?
The answer to this question may seem obvious. For many applicants it simply means entering their home address. If you are resident abroad for part of the year, you could enter

the UK postal address, as long as someone is there to collect and open important mail on your behalf. However, before entering a UK address you do need to be aware of the rules regarding claiming to be a UK or EU student. If you are a boarder, use your school address. It can easily be changed in Track, e.g. for the summer holiday. Many universities now contact you via email too, so make sure that the email address you give is appropriate and can be accessed both from school and from home.

What is my fee code?

This will let the university know how your fees are going to be paid. Usually the correct code is 02, which means that you will be applying to the local authority to be assessed for the level of tuition fees that you will pay. Other fee codes may mean, for example, that you will be charged as an independent student and pay considerably more. If you are an overseas applicant from *outside* of the EU you will **not** enter 02.

The rules about claiming to be a UK student are complex but, essentially, if your parents live in the UK and pay UK tax (and have done so for *three* years prior to your starting university), then you qualify as a UK student. Note that if you are a boarder at a UK school but do not have a parent who lives in the UK and pays UK tax, then you do not qualify. An EU student is one who lives in a country that has EU membership.

For current and up-to-date advice, contact the international student liaison team of any major UK university.

Do I need to enter any disabilities I may have?

You are obliged to answer this question but you do not have to let the university know if you are dyslexic or have another disability. However, there is **no** evidence that anything you declare will have any bearing on your application, unless it is directly related to your ability to complete the course. Indeed, if you do enter the information on the form the university will automatically alert the relevant welfare office. As a result, it may be able to offer you extra grants to purchase equipment or for one-to-one help. So my advice is to be upfront and open from the start.

What is 'Occupational Background' and do I need to disclose that I have been in care?

This is asked for Equal Opportunities purposes and refers to what job the head of your household does. The information is gathered by UCAS for statistical purposes to provide the government with a profile of applicants. It is a contentious part of the form, which is why you have the right to decline to comment in one of the drop-down boxes. There is no clear evidence that this information is used by the universities. Indeed, all the admissions tutors I spoke to when updating this book said they never even read it!

How many choices can I make?

If you are applying for a *non*-medical course, you can apply for up to five courses. You can apply for more than one course at any institution as long as the two courses are considered properly in the personal statement. For instance, you could apply to read English and English and media at the same university in the same application cycle.

You cannot apply to more than one course at either Oxford or Cambridge and you cannot apply to both universities in the same application cycle. You can apply for only *four* medicine, dentistry, veterinary medicine or veterinary science courses in one application cycle. However, you are at liberty to apply to a fifth course as a possible fall-back. A popular choice for potential medics is biomedical science.

You do not have to enter all five choices, but you ought to enter at least four. Also, to demolish this myth once and for all – the choices are not in order of preference. The computer puts them in alphabetical order.

What is a Foundation degree?

The Foundation year is designed for students who have the ability to study for a degree but don't have the qualifications to enter directly onto an honours degree. It therefore attracts many students from non-traditional educational backgrounds and under-represented groups. Nearly all major universities offer Foundation-year courses and they are well worth looking into if you do not have the right A levels or perhaps lack the academic profile that they are looking for in a direct entrant. I know of a number of students who have been accepted onto a Foundation year at prestigious universities with fairly modest A level grades. It is also a way of getting onto a medical degree or engineering degree without chemistry or physics, for instance.

Do the other universities know where I have applied?

No. The university only knows that you have applied to its institution and therefore cannot discriminate against you in any way.

How do I enter my qualifications?

Remember to include all of your qualifications (GCSEs, IGCSEs, AS, BTEC, A level or IB grades).

If you have a pass grade, please include it. For subjects that you are still studying, put the date that you expect your exam results, in most cases August, and leave the grade pending. For GCSE double awards click on GCSE double award from the options list. Include all exams for which you have a grade, even if you have retaken it, especially maths and English GCSE.

International students can enter their grades, too. UK university admissions tutors are used to receiving applications from overseas and know how to equate them with UK qualifications.

What if I do not know my exam centre number?

The exam centre number should be on your exam certificates. If in doubt, ask advice from a tutor in your school or college.

Is my employment information relevant?

In practice this is only relevant if you are a mature student with a history of full-time employment. By all means mention your summer employment history, but it is unlikely to have any bearing on most applicants' success.

How do I enter my personal statement?

You should write your personal statement in a word-processing document, spell-check it, then copy and paste it on to your UCAS Apply form. Personal statements should be approximately 550 words (4,000 characters, including spaces). Personal statements must be proofread by an appropriate third party to make sure that they meet the requirements of the course. Needless to say, they must be free from spelling, punctuation and grammatical errors.

What do I do when I have completed my form?

Ensure that you have completed all sections. You will see red ticks on page 1; if there are green dots (…) in any section box, this means that it is incomplete. Print your form off and check it for accuracy. Once your school or college tutors have agreed that your form is correct, return to your form, click that it is complete, pay the fee, answer the final security questions and send it to your referee. You cannot make any further changes after this point, unless the UCAS super-user intervenes on your behalf.

How do I pay?

This depends on your own circumstances. All payment is online by credit or debit card, unless the school or college is paying on your behalf, in which case UCAS invoices the institution for all their applicants.

What happens next?

Your school or college will normally check your form thoroughly, especially your academic results. An academic reference is attached and the form is then sent to UCAS.

On receipt of your form, UCAS sends you a welcome email and your Personal ID for tracking your application in Track. Your password is the same as the one you used to make your application. Please keep this information safe.

Your form is then sent electronically to your universities. You receive replies either directly from the university and UCAS or just from UCAS. Only offers communicated through UCAS are valid. Note, it can take months for your university to reply. You should have heard from them all by early April.

Communications with UCAS: You are asked whether you want to receive information by telephone (mobile), text message or email. If you have indicated that you are happy to receive information by any or all of these means, please ensure that your contact details are up to date. Hotmail email accounts may filter out certain messages if the junk mail filter operates efficiently; check that this cannot happen to you!

The UCAS hotline number for applicants, open in office hours during the working week, is +44 (0)371 468 0468.

What is an unconditional offer?

A small but growing number of universities now offer students an unconditional offer of a place when they think it is more than likely that the applicant will meet the grades in the summer. This is a way of guaranteeing that a place is taken, as the offer is normally made only where the student makes that institution their Firm Place, thereby making the Insurance Place redundant.

How do I reply to offers?

In short, you reply via the UCAS online Tracking system. It will not allow you to officially choose your firm choice (CF) or insurance choice (CI) until *all* your universities have responded. This can be frustrating, but be patient.

How do I find out about bursaries or financial support?

Student loans are organised via the Student Loan Company, who have a website. You register with it once you have a place at university. All universities are obliged to offer bursaries and hardship awards. They will publicise them on their websites. In addition, you can apply for scholarships or other charitable awards. The Educational Grants Advisory Service is a good place to start your search.

PART TWO

ACADEMIC PROFILES

ACCOUNTING

This profile was written using information provided by an admissions tutor at the University of Essex. The information in this profile is useful to all applicants, but some of the advice is pertinent to Essex in particular.

SUBJECT OVERVIEW

Financial information plays an important role in society because of its centrality in decision making within a variety of organisations. For example, financial information is vital in decisions such as the following.

- What effect will an increase in the price of a company's products have on its profitability?
- Will it be beneficial for a company to change its method of production?
- What will be the effect of a reduction in the funding of local government on the level of services that can be provided?
- How much additional funding does a hospital need to substantially decrease its waiting lists?

Accounting courses tend to focus both on the techniques used in accounting and the critique and evaluation of current accounting practices. Accounting degrees also cover other issues such as the appropriateness of information disclosed to shareholders, the effectiveness of regulation of auditing and the economic consequences of a change in accounting policy. Depending on the degree you study, you may also have the opportunity to study finance, management and economics.

WHAT SKILLS OR ATTRIBUTES DO ADMISSIONS TUTORS LOOK FOR IN A GOOD APPLICANT?

Applicants need to show a strong aptitude and enthusiasm for business in general, and accounting specifically. A good applicant will also be able to show an awareness of accounting and its impact in the wider world, through keeping informed of current affairs and developments in the business world and an awareness of the relationship between private and public companies and the government and regulatory bodies. Academically, students should demonstrate ability in maths, although the need for A level Maths may vary among institutions. Applicants for accounting may also be studying courses in accounting, business and economics, although these subjects are not usually compulsory entry requirements. Non-academic traits beneficial to an accounting applicant would be demonstration of an eye for detail, experience of working in a team, good communication and potential leadership skills.

WHAT DOES A GOOD PERSONAL STATEMENT LOOK LIKE?

Students should clearly state why they have chosen to study accounting and what first sparked their interest in the subject. An awareness of accountancy as a career is advantageous, so any students with work experience should highlight this. It is useful to explain what the work experience involved and why it led them to choose to apply for accounting at university. Students could also mention their current subjects studied at school/college which are relevant to the course. This is especially important if a student's current studies have inspired their choice of degree. Their current studies may also have provided skills that will be useful at university level, such as analytical skills, business knowledge and critical thinking. An awareness and understanding of current business and accounting issues is also useful to demonstrate, as is any knowledge of business practices picked up through part-time employment.

Example of a personal statement

I am applying for a degree in Accounting as I believe this degree will set me in good stead for my future career. In recent years, I have become interested in the world of commerce and industry and I believe that studying this subject at university level will help me reach my goal of becoming an accountant. I have researched this career and believe that I have the necessary skills to succeed.

At my college, all Year 12 students undertake a week's work experience in July. I arranged for mine to be at Phillips and Woodstock, a small accountancy firm in my local town. During this week I learnt that there are several elements of the accountancy profession and that the career is very diverse. Phillips and Woodstock specialise in helping small businesses with their tax assessments, and as a result I have become particularly interested in the business consultancy side of accounting. The MD, Mr Phillips, was impressed with my work and commitment and has invited me to work at the firm part time in my summer holidays. I am looking forward to the opportunity to gain more experience in my chosen career.

I am currently studying towards a BTEC Level 3 Extended Diploma in Business. The modules I have particularly enjoyed are 'Managing Information' and 'Managing a Business Project or an Event'. For the latter module, my project was based on a tender by a construction company where I took the role of estimator and tried to write a competitive tender proposal. This was a challenging and interesting task, and one that taught me the importance of expertise in a chosen field. However, it was the unit 'Introduction to Accounting' which I most enjoyed and which, in retrospect, first sparked my interest in accounting.

I have a part-time job in a roadside restaurant near to my home. Although the job can be repetitive, it has been an important exercise in self-discipline as I start work at 7 a.m. on Saturdays! I have also met many new people and become friends with some of the regulars. I try to save the money I earn from this job: university has been my long-term goal for the last year and my savings should help with the costs of studying.

I am really looking forward to going to university: partly for the social experience, but most importantly to further my studies in accounting. I believe that university will help me achieve my aim of qualifying as an accountant and perhaps one day running my own business, like Mr Phillips, or my all-time hero, Sir Alan Sugar. I would hope, however, never to be fired!

Strengths:

✓ The first sentence goes straight to the point. This implies decisiveness and commitment, and the personal statement is too short for a lengthy introduction.

✓ The student goes into a lot of detail about their work experience, which is good as it is relevant to his chosen subject and helped shape his career plans.

Weaknesses:

✗ It is a shame that the student did not go into more detail about the 'Introduction to Accounting' module, and explain how it sparked their interest in accounting, as this would be very relevant to his university application.

✗ The ending would have had more impact without the closing comment. Try to avoid flippant comments or cultural references, as admissions tutors may not understand them or share your interest in them.

 ## TOP TIPS

1 Show a knowledge of accountancy as a career as well as a subject choice

2 Mention and give details about any work experience or part-time employment that may enhance your application

3 Highlight skills you have that will be useful when studying the degree: numerical skills, team working, commitment and organisational skills

4 Show an interest in accountancy and business that exists beyond the classroom

5 Show that you are looking forward to studying this course at degree level and to the university experience

 ## THINGS TO AVOID

1 Simply stating your interests without any further explanation

2 Saying you want to be an accountant because a friend or family member is an accountant – this is not a good enough reason by itself

3 Poor spelling, punctuation and grammar – the way you present your work is just as important as the content

4 Making sweeping statements referring to 'heart's desires' and 'great passions'. It is more effective to be subtle in your enthusiasm

5 Focusing your interests purely on business or maths; if this is where your interests really lie, you should consider a joint degree!

 ## RECOMMENDED READING AND WEBSITES

▪ A. Britton and C. Waterston, *Financial Accounting*, 5th edition, Financial Times/Prentice Hall, 2009 – a useful introductory accounting textbook

- The professional accounting bodies have informative websites that contain topical information on accounting issues. For example, the Institute of Chartered Accountants in England and Wales: www.icaew.com or the website of the Association of Chartered Certified Accountants: www.accaglobal.com
- Finally, if you think you might want to train with a large firm of chartered accountants, look at the website of Deloitte as an example: www.deloitte.co.uk

I am grateful for the support of the University of Essex (www.essex.ac.uk) in the preparation of this profile. Other highly rated courses include those at the universities of Lancaster, City and Manchester.

AMERICAN STUDIES

This academic profile was written using information provided by an admissions tutor from Swansea University. The information in this profile is useful to all applicants, but please be aware that some of the advice is pertinent to that department in particular.

SUBJECT OVERVIEW

As the last global superpower, the USA has an immediate and continuing impact on all our lives, it influences our culture, our economy and our political outlook, and its foreign policy affects our future. To know and understand the nature of America, its art, culture, historical and political traditions, is to appreciate more fully the real forces driving the 21st century.

American Studies is for students with a broad-based interest in American life and American culture, especially for those with a particular interest in American history, literature, politics, film or popular culture. It is also for students who would relish the opportunity to try out many different approaches (from film analysis to exploring the American landscape), develop new skills (such as decoding advertisements or studying historical documents) and explore many disciplines, which can include art, music, communications and sociology alongside the core components of history, literature and politics and film. American Studies can also be for those who would like to experience American life at first hand, with the opportunities to study four-year degrees at a number of higher education institutions, spending a year studying, travelling and exploring the USA. Students who choose a three-year degree are likely to have the experience of being taught by professors from the USA and may have the option of spending a semester studying in the USA, depending on the course.

WHAT SKILLS OR ATTRIBUTES DO ADMISSIONS TUTORS LOOK FOR IN A GOOD APPLICANT?

American Studies does not assume any prior study of American culture, but does assume that prospective students are interested in current affairs, are willing to engage with all aspects of American culture from gangsta rap to Hollywood blockbusters to *The Great Gatsby* and are flexible and open-minded enough to cope with a wide range of teaching styles, methodological approaches and source material – whether presidential speeches, classic American novels or letters and memoirs from the American Civil War. Although most prospective students will have studied English, history, media or politics at A level, the nature of American Studies is such that most departments will be more than willing to look at any candidate who possesses a real drive and enthusiastic commitment to studying the USA. Grade requirements vary, but on average you could expect to be asked to gain between ABB and BBC (or equivalent).

WHAT DOES A GOOD PERSONAL STATEMENT LOOK LIKE?

The most important thing to demonstrate when applying for American Studies is a broad commitment to studying all aspects of American life and letters. Be as specific as you can – talk about American films you have enjoyed, American writers and novels, and aspects of American history, which especially excite you. You should also signal that you are aware of, and actively engaged with, contemporary issues – whether the presidential election, current events in the Middle East, or all sorts of other global issues. American Studies is a 'transnational' discipline, in that it also explores the impact of American policies and products on the rest of the world – thus you could also talk about issues of globalisation, foreign policy or the relationship between America, the UK and the rest of the world. Stress your flexibility and willingness to try new things – American Studies requires a great deal of energy and adaptability, as it covers so many different areas. If you have been to the US, talk about your experience – even if it was only a family trip to Orlando, you can still touch upon what aspects of America you found familiar and any parts of American life that felt to you to be strangely 'foreign'. Talk about your interests and activities in a passionate and committed manner – do not make statements, explain what you are trying to say – we are looking for well-rounded individuals with a keen interest in a wide variety of fields.

Example of a good personal statement

America is the most powerful and influential country in the world, as the phrase 'When America sneezes we all catch a cold' suggests.

✓ A good opening quote, and a clear understanding of the importance of the topic.

I am interested in studying how the USA, a global superpower, influences the culture, economy and political developments in my daily life, the United Kingdom and the rest of the world.

✓ Suggests an awareness of, and interest in, global events and current affairs.

I studied Martin Luther King and civil rights as a topic during my A level. I am enthused by his adoption of the methods of non-violence to pursue civil rights goals and his commitment to peace, non-violence and equality for all. I want to explore this further, as countries today face greater challenges for peace and stability than ever before.

✓ Specific examples really add critical weight to the statement and give an indication of the areas that the candidate is already interested in.

Not only have I learnt about America and some of its stages in history but also, due to my enjoyment of reading, I have read about it in books such as 'Little Women' and 'The Big Sleep'.

✓ The candidate covers politics, history and literature and strengthens their application by including specific titles and examples. A love of reading is very, very important!

The subjects I have chosen for A levels are English language, sociology and history. These subjects have helped to provide skills such as time organisation and structured writing.

✓ Shows a clear understanding of the study skills required.

They have also provided me with different ways in which to see the world, sociology showing the structure of society and the way people can act. In studying America it will be interesting to see the culture and society of another country and how it can change and develop. This will enable me to expand my views by challenging preconceived ideas to see whether they are right or wrong.

✓ The candidate understands that university education is about acquiring the skills to argue, discuss and debate.

I have found studying history to be stimulating and challenging and it has helped me learn how to construct my ideas and arguments through assignments and essays. This has also helped me to develop analytical and evaluating skills, which will be a great asset when studying American Studies. I'm looking forward to developing a greater depth of understanding of the world's largest superpower.

✓ Enthusiasm and energy are key factors.

I recently visited family in Arizona and experienced at first hand their culture. I want to develop this experience further through study abroad in the USA.

✓ While first-hand knowledge of America is not necessary, it does provide a basis for why the candidate might want to learn more.

> From my study and travel experience, and personal interests, spending the next three/four years learning more about American history, culture and politics and spending a year/semester living in the country will not only be interesting and fascinating but also provide me with the skills necessary for future employment in a global career.

✓ A confident, well-written and critically focused conclusion.

This is an example of a very good personal statement. The candidate sets forward their reasons for undertaking the course, and demonstrates a real sense of commitment and academic drive. They also provide a number of specific examples of areas of American culture they have already found to be stimulating and provocative, choosing these from the central areas of politics and history (civil rights) and literature (*Little Women* and *The Big Sleep*). The stress on the relationship between the USA and the UK, and, indeed, America and the rest of the world, also suggests an awareness of global issues and the importance of studying the basis and nature of American power and influence. The candidate suggests in a clear and intelligent manner how the analytical skills they have already acquired will be of enormous relevance to their chosen degree scheme. They also demonstrate a lucid understanding of what the subject is, and the degree to which it matches their own interests and enthusiasms.

Example of a poor personal statement

> The current judicial system is far from perfect, but being able to change the views of people and help in the struggle for equality is very important to me.

✗ This seems both very vague and not really relevant to American Studies – has the student applied to the right degree scheme?

> I feel that this is the perfect time to study with my good educational background and combination of business and general studies.

✗ How does this relate to American Studies? The candidate doesn't seem to be aware of the different elements that make up the scheme.

> Although I took my A levels in August 2014, I never thought about university, as I didn't think it was for me. However after nearly two years working for a telematic company I have become disillusioned in the workplace and can't imagine doing this line of work for the rest of my life, as I would like to make a difference, This is where applying for university comes in and gaining a degree as I strive for excellence.

✗ This seems very negative, as if the candidate is simply looking to escape the mundane nature of their current employment. Where is the commitment, the energy, or the imaginative enthusiasm? It is also a very badly constructed sentence.

> I am an independent, responsible and confident person who strives for perfection.

✗ Too vague – we need specific examples here.

> I can communicate with others who may find it difficult to do so. I can work independently and in a group, I can carry out tasks with the minimum of help.

✗ The candidate needs to stress their critical and analytical skills rather than specifically work-related ones.

> My hobbies include playing football, tennis, and anything sports related. As I love challenging myself and trying to become the best I possibly can in whatever activity I am pursuing.

✗ The second sentence isn't a sentence – this gives the impression that the candidate is slipshod and puts very little effort into what they do.

This candidate makes no mention of American Studies whatsoever; rather, the distinct suspicion is that the candidate, unsure of where to go next, has applied to a wide range of courses (presumably including law or criminology) and has simply written a general and very sloppy personal statement. They fail to demonstrate any awareness of the degree scheme to which they are notionally applying, and the statement is particularly lacking in any concrete examples of why they would want to undertake American Studies, or which aspects of the course (for example, film or history) they would find most interesting. The general tone is negative and unfocused; it feels as if the candidate is trapped in a dead-end job and will do anything to get out. Finally, for an individual who states that they strive for excellence, there are far too many errors in the piece – this gives the impression that the statement was cobbled together with very little thought or forward planning.

 TOP TIPS

1 Be enthusiastic: You can do anything with your life right now – what drives you to choose American Studies? Make this clear in your statement

2 Be relevant: gear your reference to specific aspects of politics, literature, history or film

3 Name names: who are your favourite writers or film-makers, what history books have you read (by whom?)

 THINGS TO AVOID

1 Writing your application as if you simply want to visit the USA as a tourist! American Studies is a challenging and academically rigorous degree

2 Silly errors, haphazard grammar and badly organised sentences – you will be spending a great deal of your time writing essays, so indicate that you possess the necessary skills

3 Over-simplifications, clichés and pat answers – a university degree is all about discussion, argument and debate

4 Assert your individuality: American Studies allows you to mould the degree scheme around your own interests and ideas, so say what these are!

5 Be aware: of the news, of global events, of the economic and cultural forces that are all around us

6 Be specific: while joint honours students will want to discuss both aspects of their degree, it is important that you stress why you're specifically interested in American Studies

4 Getting names or book titles wrong – you should name names and be specific – but make sure that you get all the names or titles of books right in the first place

5 Making a statement with no explanation

Remember, the admissions officer reviewing your application needs to be impressed by you

---

RECOMMENDED READING AND WEBSITES

- Christopher Bigsby and Howard Temperley, *A New Introduction to American Studies*, Routledge, 2005
- Read American novels, historical works and quality newspapers for current affairs in the USA
- British Association for American Studies: www.baas.ac.uk
- American Studies Resource Centre at Liverpool John Moores University: www.americansc.org.uk

I am grateful for the support of Swansea University (www.swansea.ac.uk/american) in the preparation of this profile. Other highly rated courses include those at the universities of Warwick, Manchester, Liverpool, East Anglia and Lancaster.

ARCHAEOLOGY AND ANTHROPOLOGY

This academic profile was written using information provided by admissions tutors at the University of Southampton and focuses on archaeology as a single honours discipline. The information in this profile is useful to all applicants, but please be aware that some of the advice is pertinent to that department in particular.

SUBJECT OVERVIEW

Archaeology is most commonly found in a humanities faculty and is commonly taught as either a single honours degree or jointly with subjects such as anthropology (the study of human development and society), geography or classical history. It is a subject that provides the opportunity to uncover past peoples and their worlds. From their material remains, you can find out about their daily lives: what they ate, what they wore and the kinds of landscapes they lived in. You can also find out about the 'big questions' about how society was organised, the scale of trade and exchange, belief structures and technology. Archaeology offers a unique blend of humanities and science, practical and theoretical.

Most courses offer a work placement option, where undergraduates spend time with qualified archaeologists in the field. Many of the fieldwork projects, which are a required element of the degree course, are overseas. Current research field projects at Southampton include Nevis (Caribbean), Calabria (Italy), Andalucía (Spain) and Namibia (Southern Africa).

Archaeology is not just a vocational subject. Graduates go on to a wide range of careers and find that their knowledge can be applied to work in local government planning, in historical preservation bodies, such as the National Trust, or in museums.

By studying archaeology, you will acquire some key skills sought by employers, such as time management, problem solving, team-work, project management and cultural awareness. Above all, you will learn to communicate ideas and enthusiasm to a wide range of audiences in a way that is relevant and understandable.

Work placements and fieldwork opportunities reflect the dedication departments have to embedding employability in students throughout the degree experience. A balanced mix of practical and theoretical learning means graduates are equipped with a comprehensive skill-set upon completing the degree. From team-working to problem solving, many are transferable. The destinations of archaeology and anthropology graduates are as rich and varied as the courses on offer.

WHAT SKILLS OR ATTRIBUTES DO ADMISSIONS TUTORS LOOK FOR IN A GOOD APPLICANT?

Archaeology A level is still taught by only a small number of colleges, so we do not have any specific subject requirements, and our students come from a diversity of paths: either all sciences, all arts or a combination. For archaeological science and combined honours programmes, we do look for a good grade in specific appropriate subjects, and this would be true of most other departments. That being said, students who do study archaeology to A level would need to highlight what aspects of their work they have found most interesting and discuss their fieldwork opportunities and coursework plans.

Note: some courses are BSc and others BA. BSc courses have greater scientific content and, as such, departments offering this option, may ask for biology or chemistry A level.

More important is that you should be able to demonstrate an interest in finding out about the past, whether from excavation or museum experience, or from family holidays visiting British castles, or the ruins of Pompeii. We look for a questioning mind and enthusiasm, as evidenced by a good academic track record at A level and GCSE, and performance at interview. GCSE Maths at grade B is commonly expected, to cope with the statistical elements of the course.

As archaeology is largely about team-work, we also look for ability to work as part of a team: you do not have to be the life and soul of the party, but you do need to be willing to participate and join in.

WHAT DOES A GOOD PERSONAL STATEMENT LOOK LIKE?

You should use your personal statement as an opportunity to show that you are interested in the study of the past. Only approximately 25% of applicants will have studied archaeology at AS or A2 level, so why do you want to study it at university? What stirred your interest – was it a childhood visit to an ancient monument, or a particular TV programme? What have you done to further that interest – visiting more sites in Britain and abroad, reading specific books, taking part in an excavation or work experience in a museum? What skills do you have from your GCSEs and A levels, or from extra-curricular activities, that prepare you for an archaeology degree? If you are applying for a combined honours degree, why do you want to do that particular combination?

 TOP TIPS

1 Say what it is that excites you about the past

2 Mention specific sites and museums you have visited

 THINGS TO AVOID

1 Plagiarising your statement by downloading it from the web or copying it word for word from a book

3 If you are applying for a combined honours degree, say why you want to study both subjects together

4 If you have an interest in a particular aspect of archaeology – for example, Romans or animal bones – mention it

5 Be positive

6 Make sure you present yourself in as compelling and interesting way as you can

2 Applying for combined honours in archaeology and history and then only talking about how interested you are in history and failing to mention archaeology – we assume you will not get the grades for a history degree and are using the combined honours as a back door into the single honours

3 Spelling and grammatical mistakes in your personal statement

4 Saying anything about yourself that is not true – we usually find out at interview

5 Including left-field archaeological ideas – the Pyramids were not built by aliens!

RECOMMENDED READING AND WEBSITES

- Council for British Archaeology: http://new.archaeologyuk.org
- Current Archaeology: www.archaeology.co.uk
- Creative and Cultural Skills: www.ccskills.org.uk
- Chartered Institute for Archaeologists: www.archaeologists.net
- Society for the Protection of Ancient Buildings: www.spab.org.uk

I am grateful for the support of the University of Southampton (www.southampton.ac.uk/archaeology) in the preparation of this profile. Other highly rated courses include those at the universities of Durham, York, Sheffield, Cambridge and Oxford.

BIOLOGICAL SCIENCES

This profile was written using information provided by an admissions tutor at the University of Essex. The information in this profile is useful to all applicants, but some of the advice is pertinent to Essex in particular.

SUBJECT OVERVIEW

Biological sciences is a broad-based degree course that can cover many topics, ranging from cell and molecular biology to genetics, marine and freshwater biology, biodiversity and applied ecology. Most biological sciences degrees will provide a broad and balanced knowledge of modern biology, centred on the organism but including molecular, genetic, cellular and population aspects, and the opportunity to specialise in particular areas. Biological sciences courses will cover field and laboratory skills and training in scientific methods as well as theoretical knowledge.

WHAT SKILLS OR ATTRIBUTES DO ADMISSIONS TUTORS LOOK FOR IN A GOOD APPLICANT?

Applicants should be able to demonstrate a firm knowledge and serious interest in biology and issues related to the subject, such as stem cell therapy, vaccines, conservation, evolution and climate change. As biological sciences is such a large area of study that covers many topics, universities tend to offer the opportunity to specialise within the course. Therefore, if an applicant can express an interest in a certain area of biology, this can be advantageous (but make sure the institutions you are applying to offer the specialism you are looking for!). Most biological sciences courses will require previous study of biology to A level standard or equivalent.

WHAT DOES A GOOD PERSONAL STATEMENT LOOK LIKE?

Example of a personal statement

From an early age I have been fascinated by biology. I can clearly recall spending time in the garden with my grandfather looking at bugs and creepy crawlies. As I grew up, my affinity with the natural world developed and studying biology at university is the next step on my journey.

I have had the most amazing gap-year experience protecting the lora turtles of Costa Rica from human poachers and beach erosion. As a volunteer on the programme I was able to help with research and conservation work, such as night patrolling, working in the hatcheries, collecting eggs, rescuing and tagging turtles and helping the baby turtles get to the sea! This opportunity has enabled me to grow as a person in many ways. It certainly has been the best preparation possible for university life, as I have acquired all kinds of skills that will be essential for a new life away from friends and family.

A level biology has certainly provided me with an excellent grounding and I am confident that I have a real aptitude for this challenging discipline. I have enjoyed all of the modules taken, especially ecosystems, as we had to consider the dynamics of such systems and look into human activities that impact on them. I particularly like doing practical work and look forward to being able to gain experience with more developed pieces of apparatus at university.

I have held several positions of responsibility. During my final year at school I was appointed to the position of senior prefect. This was a great honour and I learnt many new skills, including public speaking. At college I continued this type of responsibility by being nominated student voice rep. This position required me to attend various meetings with different types of people, including the Board of Governors. I was the voice for all 2,000 students at our college.

I am an eager table tennis player and regularly compete at county level. I find it to be an excellent form of exercise for the body and mind! I am keen to try out different sports when I reach university because it will be the perfect way to make new friends and stay healthy. The Duke of Edinburgh Award scheme is also something that I am involved in and I have completed bronze, silver and gold awards. I am hoping to be involved in promoting the award scheme to young people in the future as I have really benefited from it and would like to be able to share my experience with others.

Strengths:

✓ It can be good to talk about past experiences that have sparked interest in the subject. However, be careful not to go off on a tangent and write more than is necessary!

✓ The gap-year experience is very relevant here and the student's enthusiasm is obvious; enthusiasm for a subject is very important.

Weaknesses:

✗ This statement has a strong beginning and middle but concludes far too abruptly; you should always finish your statement with an enthusiastic and memorable ending.

✗ This student ends by talking about his Duke of Edinburgh achievements, which, though interesting, probably isn't the main reason why they are applying to university. It is preferable to conclude your personal statement by talking about your chosen subject and/or your eagerness to go to university.

 TOP TIPS

1 Display a strong enthusiasm for biology and explain why the subject interests you

2 Provide details about the courses you are currently studying and skills and knowledge that will help you in higher education

3 Show an interest in specialising during your degree

4 Discuss any practical experience you have had, such as work experience or field trips

 THINGS TO AVOID

1 Simply stating your interests without any further explanation

2 Being negative in any part of your personal statement creates an overall negative impression of you – always be positive!

3 Describing your activities, hobbies and interests but not giving any further details about them or what you have gained from them

4 Neglecting to talk about biological sciences or why it interests you – this is the most important information for us!

5 If your extra-curricular activities or hobbies are at all relevant to biology, do highlight this. Otherwise, highlight the transferable skills you have gained from these activities

5 Showing a lack of understanding or awareness of the impact of biology/ecology/conservation, etc. in the outside world

RECOMMENDED READING AND WEBSITES

- University of Essex Biological Sciences website: www.essex.ac.uk/bs
- Royal Society of Biology: www.rsb.org.uk for links to careers advice
- British Ecological Society: www.britishecologicalsociety.org
- Biochemical Society: www.biochemistry.org
- The Royal Society: www.royalsociety.org – follow the Journals page
- Institute of Biomedical Science: www.ibms.org

I am grateful to the University of Essex for its help in preparing this profile. Other highly rated courses can be found at the universities of Cambridge, York, Oxford, Leicester and St Andrews.

BUSINESS, BANKING, MANAGEMENT AND ACTUARIAL SCIENCE

This academic profile is a composite of information provided by admissions tutors at both Aston University and City University London. The information is useful to all applicants, but some of the advice is pertinent to Aston or City in particular.

SUBJECT OVERVIEW

The practice of business and management (and all the other specialisms, such as accounting, marketing and economics) is a varied and fascinating subject and taking place around us every day. The globalised business and financial world and power of brands, finance, marketing, consumer behaviour, large organisations and multinationals, along with the importance of entrepreneurship and forward thinking means that a business degree is useful in many careers. Many business degrees include a fantastic opportunity to take a placement year in industry/commerce or to work or study abroad as part of the course. Business students are a massively varied group of people, often from all over the world, offering lots of new perspectives, friends and future contacts. Many students go on to complete accountancy exams or take the MBA course at a business school.

Business studies and management are essentially practice-oriented subjects that focus on the organisation and its operations. These degrees are often BSc or MSc, with an expectation that an applicant's maths skills will be sound. Many, but not all, will require maths at A level or IB. All will expect a good pass at GCSE in maths. Some courses are three years and others four with a work placement built in. These four-year courses tend to be more popular and hence have higher academic entry requirements.

Business studies analyses the key functions that most organisations need to develop in order to survive and prosper, whether commercial, not-for-profit or public agencies. It includes a diverse range of subjects which have developed a range of theories and models, requiring differing techniques and skills. Management is both a practical skill and a body of theory that draws on a multitude of thinkers who have written on a wide range of aspects of the subject over the last two centuries. Most courses include an introduction to financial accounting, law for business, marketing, business operations, strategic management, information technology and some applied economics modules.

Banking and finance is the study of the financial markets and the role of banking within that. The recent turmoil in these markets underlines the enormous importance of this sector to a modern economy. The subject focuses on different types of financial markets, institutions and their roles, as well as security analysis and valuation. Change is a feature of the subject in response to evolving market conditions and theory development by academic and practitioner researchers. Models and theories tend to be quantitative. Students would be expected to handle the applications of these models. As such, a minimum of an A level in maths would be a requirement of most courses.

The BSc (Hons) Banking and International Finance provides you with the skills required to operate in the competitive world of financial markets, in the key areas including: financial institutions, commercial and investment banking, bank and corporate risk management, international banking, banking regulation, fixed income, derivatives, international finance, corporate finance and applied economics.

The actuarial science degree prepares students for a career as an actuary or in any other area involving finance and risk. Actuaries are employed to assess risks in a variety of business situations and advise their clients or employers as to the likely costs associated with the various possible outcomes. Probability and statistics are at the heart of their professional expertise. Students will learn to use and apply the relevant mathematical models, probability and statistical theory and information technology. Communication skills are also prized by the actuarial profession. Maths at A level is a standard requirement for entry to all well-regarded courses. The career path as an actuary is higher paid and for that reason standard entry requirements tend to be high.

WHAT SKILLS OR ATTRIBUTES DO ADMISSIONS TUTORS LOOK FOR IN A GOOD APPLICANT?

All degrees require good numeracy, literacy and reasoning skills.

We need to see evidence of commitment to a business and management degree, for instance a demonstrable interest in the business world. A good candidate would have an awareness of recent issues in the UK economy that are relevant, for instance the recent upheaval in the sub-prime market and its impact on banking and finance. Academic skills might be illustrated by a business studies or economics A level or equivalent, but this is not always obligatory. Maths is another skill that is relevant, although the need for an A level will vary from course to course. A good candidate will show an awareness of globalisation, customer focus, organisations and how they work, the importance of brands and marketing, finance and economics. A candidate interested in banking and finance would need to put forward a case as to why they want to specialise at this stage. No reason not to, but this ambition needs to be explained – to make money is not a good response! Particular awareness of the recent and continuing banking crisis and its impact on the world economy would be expected in a personal statement.

Non-academic skills might include good communication and team-work skills, evidence of leadership or putting forward new ideas – for example, in part-time or voluntary work. Initiative is rewarded, so show evidence of projects you have initiated, such as student magazines or student-led fundraising schemes. The Young Enterprise and Duke of Edinburgh Award schemes are other means of showing these attributes.

Actuarial science requires a high level of mathematical knowledge on entry (A at A level or equivalent). Those who have good A level scores in other subjects but have failed to get the requisite mathematical score are directed to an additional one-year pre-university Foundation course to bring their mathematical skills up to an acceptable level. Students who do well on the actuarial science degree are those with a genuine passion for mathematics and who enjoy applying their mathematical skills to solving real-world problems. Students also need an interest in the financial world. The actuarial science degree is demanding and so students who are well organised and self-motivated are also well placed to succeed.

WHAT DOES A GOOD PERSONAL STATEMENT LOOK LIKE?

Your personal statement is a key part of your UCAS application form. Most good business schools in the UK receive a lot of applications, many of which are from applicants who meet or are predicted to meet the academic entry requirements, so it is essential that you write a good personal statement in order to stand out from the competition.

Make it clear and concise, clearly state why you want to study business, management or another related course. Make it clear what your interests are and your specific subjects at school/college – for example, business, accounting, geography, economics – which you feel are relevant and worth talking about. Emphasise the relevant skills you have learnt and the books, newspapers and magazines that you have read to extend your understanding of the subject. You can see good examples below. You are encouraged to refer to demonstrable interests that you might have in the business world. In this regard, the Young Enterprise scheme and other similar schemes are useful. Reference to current issues affecting business is always welcome.

Admissions officers realise that many applicants will also apply to other institutions and may still be making up their mind between a couple of subjects. You will not therefore be disadvantaged if your personal statement states that you are interested in studying BSc Management or another discipline such as sociology. As long as you then explain what it is about those two very different courses that appeals to you, this will not be held against you.

Finally, in order to optimise your chance of being offered a place, the best piece of advice we can give you is to submit a neat and complete application. A personal statement with several spelling or grammatical errors does not engender much confidence in your writing skills. Competition is very high at top business schools, so do not undermine your chances with lazy spelling or poor grammar. Ask a parent or teacher to proofread it carefully.

TOP TIPS

1 Emphasise the skills that you have already acquired that are both academic and non-academic

2 Mention any work experience, business experience and/or taster courses that you have attended that may enhance your application

3 Good personal statements show that the applicant has researched into their chosen subject and knows a little about the course content or study options available. Read prospectuses and websites – business courses are different across the UK in how and what they teach and specialise in, and in how you are assessed. Your understanding of these needs to be reflected in your personal statements

4 Do your research in plenty of time during March–July of Year 12 or equivalent – ready to complete and send off your UCAS form well before Christmas in Year 13 or equivalent. Early research also helps to establish enough time to prepare your statement properly

5 Explain gap-year plans clearly, and where possible show how they will benefit you as a potential student

6 University study is very different to school or college life. The admissions team will be looking for examples within your personal statement that show that you have transferable skills which will equip you for success on your degree course

THINGS TO AVOID

1 Repetition

2 Unsubstantiated claims that you could not defend in an interview

3 Poor spelling, punctuation and grammar. Check and read your personal statement carefully. You would be surprised how many errors we see that are the result of lazy proofreading or reliance on spell checkers

4 Sweeping generalisations, such as 'I have always been passionate about a career in …'. This is rarely true!

5 Choosing a university or particular course just because it is high in the league tables or your parents/teachers think it makes them look good – choose a university because you think the course content, reputation, graduate employability, teaching and social facilities are right for you. If appropriate, you might indicate that you have done this in the body of your statement. Do not mention individual universities, but do indicate in general terms that you have done your research

6 Assuming that we know all about you. We can't check you out on Facebook or YouTube – all we have is the UCAS form. So use it to sell yourself!

7 Using humour or crass statements on your personal statement – keep it concise, serious and realistic but positive

RECOMMENDED READING AND WEBSITES

- Carly Roberts, *Getting into Business & Economics Courses*, Trotman Education, 2015
- Philip Coggan, *The Money Machine: How the City Works*, Penguin, 2015 – a great introductory read for those interested in finance and banking
- Christopher Stoakes, *Know the City*, Christopher Stoakes Ltd, 2015 – a very good guide, updated annually and well reviewed on Amazon
- *The Financial Times*: www.ft.com – an excellent source for business economics. Also contains a portfolio service for you to build your own virtual share portfolio and track your wealth
- *The Economist*: www.economist.com – web version of the weekly newspaper – lots of political economy, with a libertarian slant. Some articles are only available for those with subscription
- Business/finance pages of papers like the *Guardian*, *The Times*, the *Independent* and the *Daily Telegraph* to get a range of perspectives
- Marketing Week: www.marketingweek.co.uk; The World Bank: www.worldbank.org – a detailed starting point for information and analysis of development issues
- Oneworld: www.oneworld.net – source of information on world economic events, giving an alternative view to that of the World Bank and International Monetary Fund (IMF)
- www.actuaries.org.uk – the website for the actuarial society. The starting point for anyone wanting to get into this lucrative but demanding area of business
- The Bank of England: www.bankofengland.co.uk – a good source of information about macroeconomic policy in the UK, specially designed for A level students
- Association of Chartered Accountants: www.accaglobal.com/uk
- Institute of Consulting: www.iconsulting.org.uk
- Chartered Management Institute: www.managers.org.uk
- National Enterprise Network: www.nationalenterprisenetwork.org

I am grateful for the support received from Aston University (www.aston.ac.uk) in the preparation of this profile. Other highly rated courses include those at the universities of Oxford, Leicester, Imperial College, St Andrews and Warwick.

CLASSICS

Classics, classical studies, ancient history, classical archaeology

This academic profile was written using information provided by an admissions tutor at King's College London. The information is useful to all applicants, but some of the advice is pertinent to King's College London in particular.

SUBJECT OVERVIEW

To start, let me assure you that you do not need to be posh to study Classics. This is a media myth! Departments admit from all backgrounds and age ranges. So if you are interested in Rome, Greece or the ancient world, then just go for it!

The cultures of the ancient world, embracing everything from the palaces of Bronze Age Crete to Roman cities on the African frontier, are fascinating to study in their own right. But because classical texts and art have significantly influenced thought, literature and politics since ancient times, they also offer a master key to understanding much of Western culture.

Classics, classical studies, ancient history and classical archaeology make up a family of degree programmes offering different avenues of approach to ancient cultures, via their languages and literature (in the original or in translation), their political, military and cultural history, their material remains and their effects on later times.

It is a misconception that you must have studied Latin or Greek at A level to be accepted onto a course. That being said, many students have, so this may be an advantage. Do check carefully what each department expects. If the emphasis is on history and not language, you are less likely to need Latin A level.

Although each individual programme has its own specific focus and methods, they also offer the possibility of combining a diverse range of subjects in one course. This makes for great transferable skills and good graduates in Classics often find themselves in good jobs. They enter employment across a range of careers, including finance, journalism, law, teaching and the civil service.

WHAT SKILLS OR ATTRIBUTES DO ADMISSIONS TUTORS LOOK FOR IN A GOOD APPLICANT?

As a good Classics applicant you will have the same general skills and attributes as any good humanities applicant: enthusiasm, self-motivation, a desire to learn, an appetite both for different perspectives and for challenging questions. The King's College London admissions team hopes to see applicants who enjoy independently exploring new topics, whether in the library, the museum or the field; people who want to engage with new problems and techniques, and to get behind the clichés of mass-media versions of ancient myth and conflict. This is an approach that will be mirrored in similar departments elsewhere.

Because of their different angles of approach, the different degree programmes within Classics do not all call for exactly the same skills and strengths; there are variations in emphasis from one university department to another. In particular, it is a good idea for applicants without an ancient language to check what quantity of work in classical Greek or Latin a particular programme is going to expect.

Departments that require compulsory language work from all their students want to see evidence that you have some aptitude for and interest in learning languages. If you have been lucky enough to acquire ancient languages at school, bear in mind that university assessment will require more extended commentary and essay writing in the English language in all topics, so the ability to write as well as translate fluently is key. You may well be tested in this skill if you are asked to attend an interview.

Departments recruiting for degrees in classical archaeology will also prefer candidates with an ability to look carefully at visual evidence and to produce some ideas about how material objects may be used to reconstruct the ancient world. Admissions staff for both archaeology and ancient history will be interested in how analytically you can think about evidence and piece together your ideas based on it.

Depending on the university's balance between individual and group teaching, universities may look for evidence that you will be a responsive student, willing to voice your opinion in a group, or to discuss your ideas with the lecturer and with fellow students. Your key qualities will be enthusiasm and motivation.

WHAT DOES A GOOD PERSONAL STATEMENT LOOK LIKE?

Remember whom you are talking to in your personal statement: the admissions tutor is a member of the academic staff whose job it is to let in students whom s/he thinks s/he and her/his colleagues will find interesting and enjoyable to teach and have in their department. So sell yourself first and foremost as a sparky, intelligent, interestingly teachable enthusiast for the subject(s) you are applying for. Everything else is secondary, however brilliant your sporting record, your Young Enterprise achievements or your tap-dancing.

Try to be individual without going over the top. If you suspect lots of other people are going to be saying what you are thinking of saying (for example, 'I've always been interested in the ancient world, ever since I first opened a book of Greek myths'), then either don't say it, or find some individual slant (for example, a particular myth and the problem it sets you, or the insight it gives you into the world of the Greeks). Try to avoid clichés and verdicts that sound as if you are delivering them only because you think it's expected, or because that's what you were told to say in an A level essay ('In my reading I have much enjoyed exploring the contrast between Catullus' coarse invective and the rhetorical wit of Ovid'). You should aim to demonstrate your skills and interests rather than just stating them, through specific examples.

Show that you have got a sense of the questions that are there to be asked, and the new territory you will be able to explore at university (but without becoming just mistily aspirational – this will just put admissions tutors off). It is fine to talk about your extra-curricular activities and successes, but try to make sure that what you say helps to show that you have the kinds of skill (like time management) that will also help you to make a success of your studies and be an asset to the department.

If you have not been able to study the ancient world at school (for example, AS or A level work in ancient history or classical civilisation), it is important to show through other evidence that you are a suitable and interesting candidate. Demonstrate that you have an intelligent interest from activity outside formal study. This might include reading of Greek and Roman history and literature (preferably including ancient texts in translation, rather than only modern works of popular history); visits to archaeological sites and museums; and interest in ancient remains in Greece and Italy (and other relevant parts of the world, even if you have not managed to visit yet). Mention specifics – works of ancient literature, or of historical analysis, or places that you have found particularly intriguing – and say why. These may be followed up in interview, so make sure that your interest is genuine!

You should also try to explain how the work you have done at school, even if not directly focused on the ancient world, has nevertheless equipped you, in terms of approach, to tackle the ancient world. You do not have to apologise for not (yet) knowing any Latin or Greek – most students in classical studies, ancient history and classical archaeology will be starting in exactly the same position.

Your personal statement is also the place to explain anything unusual in your qualifications so far. If you need to, give good reasons to show that your formal results so far give a misleading picture of your real abilities. Tutors know that accidents happen in exams, and are very ready to listen to well-documented explanations.

Examples from specific personal statements

From a candidate who has studied ancient languages at school:

> I have loved Latin since I began it at the age of nine.

✓ It is encouraging that you still enjoy ancient languages after lengthy study, and your background in the subject will stand you in good stead for university. You could add that you have been looking in new directions for your university career. What authors have you read and would you like to go on to read? How do you think they may fit into the wider history of the ancient world? Are there any themes (death and mourning, involvement in politics, descriptions of remote places) in the texts that you have read that you would like to explore further?

From a candidate who has little school background in the study of the ancient world:

> My interest was first sparked by the myths of Greece and Rome ... I am very interested in ancient warfare and the conquests of Alexander the Great.

✗ Your attention has, understandably, been attracted by certain prominent stories and figures and this is appreciated by the admissions tutor. But if you're considering studying this at university, try to contextualise the images you have of the ancient world more. What have you read in ancient texts about warfare? What further questions might you go on to ask about Alexander the Great? Is there a course at your preferred university that covers this period and which will offer you more?

From a candidate interested in classical archaeology:

> In my gap year, I will be studying for a Foundation course in art at X Art School. I am interested in all periods of art history and I would particularly like to study the relationship between ancient sculpture and Renaissance art.

✓ Coming to the study of archaeology with a background in art, rather than science, can produce interesting and equally valid approaches. Your dedication to a whole year of fine art study will suggest to the admissions tutor that you might work well with visual analysis and respond in interesting ways to the ancient evidence. There can be very different kinds of archaeological study, however, and an interviewer might be interested in to what extent you're aware of this. An interest in art history would also be balanced by the practical experience of a British dig, for which you could volunteer.

TOP TIPS

1 Be intelligently enthusiastic

2 Make sure you know the details of the programmes you are applying for and that this is reflected in the body of the text

3 Keep your personal statement focused on what will make you a rewarding student for your chosen subject

4 Read through what you have written and correct it where necessary

5 Back up what you say about yourself with evidence from extended reading, fieldwork or other sources. Be prepared to defend what you say if called to interview

6 If your choice of subject is a recent one and you have not had years to construct a relevant extra-curricular CV, you can provide an equally encouraging and impressive substitute in your personal statement by writing in detail about relevant background reading and by describing the further preparatory study you may undertake – perhaps a summer school, independent language study (with course book), visits to local Roman sites or more exotic climes or volunteer work in a museum or site. The more detailed and worked-out these plans are, the better

 THINGS TO AVOID

1 Being too vague in your explanations of interest – try to get to the point quickly and back it up

2 Parroting second-hand opinions

3 Going on at great length about activities and achievements that are irrelevant to your chosen course

4 Poor spelling, punctuation and grammar. Make sure that the statement is proofread by someone other than you and someone with a sound knowledge of grammar and punctuation too!

5 Pretending to have read books that you have not had time to read yet – some applicants will be called for interview and you could be caught out!

6 Saying anything that you could not defend face to face

 RECOMMENDED READING AND WEBSITES

■ Mary Beard *A Very Short Introduction to Classics*, Oxford University Press, 2000

■ University of Oxford: www.classics.ox.ac.uk

- Durham University: www.dur.ac.uk/classics
- University of Warwick: www2.warwick.ac.uk/services/library/subjects/arts/classics

I am grateful for the support I received from King's College London (www.kcl.ac.uk/artshums/depts/classics) in preparing this profile. Other highly rated courses include those at the universities of Oxford, Cambridge, Durham, Edinburgh and Exeter.

COMPUTER SCIENCE

This profile was written using information from an admissions tutor at Royal Holloway, University of London. The information is useful to all applicants, but some of the advice is pertinent to that department in particular.

SUBJECT OVERVIEW

Computers, the internet, the web and other digital technologies continue to transform the economy, the world of finance and many other aspects of society. This digital revolution is accelerating and will play a key role in shaping the future. Computer science lies at the heart of this transformation: it studies how any sort of information, whether it is music or biological sequence data, can be represented and processed digitally. Demand for good computer science graduates has never been higher: a degree in computer science equips you for many challenging and, often, very well-paid jobs in energy-providing companies, companies producing computer games, telecoms, banks and other financial companies. Research by the eSkills sector skills council for information technology (IT) and telecoms shows that the employment market for IT careers is growing five times faster than the general economy; every year 140,000 new entrants to the IT and telecoms workforce are needed.

Computer science is an excellent preparation for many careers, both technical and non-technical, throughout commerce and industry because students acquire intellectual discipline and practical project-completion skills which are highly valued, as well as specific technical skills that are in great demand. These include:

- the ability to analyse complex problems
- the ability to acquire the skills needed to solve problems and to design and implement solutions
- programming skills, including networking and databases

- data-analysis skills
- communication skills
- the ability to work in a team
- leadership skills and management ability
- literacy and numeracy
- presentation skills.

WHAT SKILLS OR ATTRIBUTES DO ADMISSIONS TUTORS LOOK FOR IN A GOOD APPLICANT?

Computer science is a hard but rewarding discipline. Admissions tutors generally tend to look for students who have some sort of technical or mathematical background. Students without an A level (or equivalent) in a technical subject like maths, physics or computing often struggle with the more abstract thinking required in computer science. Many first-year students have no previous experience with programming, but if students have some programming experience in a language, for example Python or Visual Basic, that is not just a markup or scripting language, that is a good selling point. Tutors also tend to look for some interest in or enthusiasm for computers, even if this is quite general.

In terms of academic qualifications, departments vary and you need to do your research. However, as a general rule the better departments will expect grades of between AAB and BBB and most good candidates will have studied A level Maths and/or Computing. Physics A level and the other mainstream sciences are also preferred. However, do your research carefully to ascertain what each department requires.

Tutors want students who have the maturity and self-discipline to cope with the more autonomous nature of university life; students need to be able to manage their time and balance the demands of the different courses. Students also need to be problem solvers; they need to be curious and independent minded. Students can show they have these personal qualities through the range of their extra-curricular activities or part-time work.

WHAT DOES A GOOD PERSONAL STATEMENT LOOK LIKE?

Example of a good personal statement

This statement is a composite of various personal statements:

I have always been very interested in computers. When I was a child, I would often take things apart to see how they work. When I was 10 years old, I was given a computer for my birthday, and while I started off just playing games and so on with it, I soon became more interested in trying to understand how it worked. At first I would just write little macros in Visual Basic to do useful things, but then I taught myself Java, and have written some simple games using this as part of my school computer club. I am also very interested in graphics and Photoshopping pictures to make them more interesting. I have made several websites using PHP and CSS, and I spend a lot of time reading about computers on the web and in magazines. My current computer I built myself from parts, which was a very educational experience, especially as it didn't work to start off and I had to figure out why.

I have a part-time job at PC World, where I work as part of a team providing technical support for customers. My hobbies include playing the piano, and I have achieved Grade 5. I play sometimes in a band with some friends. My other main interest is sport, especially cricket. I have been part of the school team for several years.

Academically, I have always been interested in maths, and with my love of computers, computer science seems a natural choice. I chose maths and physics as two of my A levels, but not computing as I didn't enjoy ICT much at GCSE level, because the course focused just on using programs rather than making them.

I am hard working and well organised, and think I will be able to cope well with the demands of a hard degree like CS: I am looking forward to the challenges of university life, and I want to get a job working in IT when I graduate.

✓ This is a good personal statement, as it gives some reasons why the student wants to study computer science, and illustrates their enthusiasm for the subject with concrete examples. The student shows they have self-discipline, take part in a range of activities and have a serious interest in computing.

 TOP TIPS

1 Make sure that you emphasise your ability in the technical or mathematical subjects

2 If you enjoy puzzles, chess, card games (such as poker or bridge) and mental-arithmetic puzzles such as Sudoku, let us know

3 If you have knowledge of programming, even at a fairly basic level, please let us know and tell us about programs you have written

 THINGS TO AVOID

1 Spelling and punctuation mistakes

2 Lying or plagiarism

3 Underselling your achievements

4 Telling us you are only interested in gaming – you may be, but this should be counterbalanced with your other interests

5 Not showing an interest in things other than computing – we want rounded applicants, not just those who sit in front of a screen all day!

4 If you are studying computer science at school, tell us what you particularly enjoyed that led you to apply for a degree-level qualification. Read one of the suggested books and mention what you learnt from the book

5 Sell yourself in a compelling and interesting manner: write clearly and concisely

RECOMMENDED READING AND WEBSITES

- Martin Ford, *The Rise of Robots: Technology and the Threat of Mass Unemployment*, Oneworld Publications, 2015
- David Harel and Yishai Feldman, *Algorithmics: The Spirit of Computing*, Springer, 2014
- Nell Dale and John Lewis, *Computer Science Illuminated*, Jones and Bartlett Publishers, 2010
- Eric S. Raymond, *The Cathedral and the Bazaar: Musings on Linux and Open Source*, O'Reilly Media, 2001
- Cliff Stoll, *The Cuckoo's Egg: Tracking a Spy through the Maze of Computer Espionage*, Pocket Books, 2007
- BCS, the Chartered Institute for IT: www.bcs.org
- The Tech Partnership: www.thetechpartnership.com
- Institution of Analysts and Programmers (IAP): www.iap.org.uk/main

I am grateful for the support of Royal Holloway, University of London in the production of this profile. (www.royalholloway.ac.uk). Other highly rated courses include those at the universities of Imperial College London, Lancaster, Oxford, Bristol and Queen Mary.

DRAMA AND THEATRE STUDIES

This academic profile was written using information provided by an admissions tutor at Royal Holloway, University of London. The information is useful to all applicants, but some of the advice is pertinent to that department in particular.

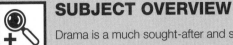

SUBJECT OVERVIEW

Drama is a much sought-after and stimulating degree programme. At university, the study of performance often combines theory with practice. Drama is important because the idea of performance pervades all aspects of public and private life. Performance is about communication, and we live in a society where communication, be it with people in the same room or over the internet, is more important than ever. Studying drama at university explores human interaction both in the present and in the past, in familiar and unfamiliar cultural settings. To study drama is to explore an ancient art form of social practice, but one that remains fundamentally important to the contemporary world. Drama as a form of cultural practice enables us to discern who we are and how we relate to others.

Students explore these ideas through a variety of modes of study, active as well as sedentary, group based as well as individual, spoken as well as written, and analytical as well as creative.

The study of drama and theatre provides you with useful life and employment skills, because of its emphasis on both individual and team work, the planning and managing of projects, and exploring the implications of rigorous research in imaginative and creative ways.

A degree programme aims to teach as full a range of skills as possible, from the academic expertise of research and theoretical reading and writing to practical theatre skills. Students develop an inquisitive and questioning attitude to all aspects of the discipline. Specifically, students will gain skills in a variety of communications: writing traditional essays, presenting seminars, listening to peers' presentations and being able to pinpoint arguments that need further teasing out, as well as presenting performance work and mounting installations. Written skills in essay writing, logbook entries, review writing and bibliographic skills are also taught and assessed. Analytical skills in close textual reading, theoretical application and performance analysis are also gained. The skills of a drama graduate are easily transferable to other environments and are therefore very highly sought after by employers.

WHAT SKILLS OR ATTRIBUTES DO ADMISSIONS TUTORS LOOK FOR IN A GOOD APPLICANT?

Admissions tutors look for someone who has the ability to question. They are not looking for 'knowledge' of the subject because that merely tells them about the teaching that a candidate has received up to this point and not about the candidate themselves. Above all else, they are looking for potential.

Candidates need to demonstrate an interest in theatre, but this does not have to be in performing. Many university courses in drama are not concerned with developing acting abilities but, rather, with fostering skills in group work, analysis, cultural engagement and the bringing together of theoretical and practical exploration. They are ideal for candidates who have a broad interest in the subject but are not yet sure in which direction they want to take their career.

Admissions tutors like candidates who are good group members: this might be shown socially by the range of activities the student undertakes. They are also looking to match students to courses: for example, someone who wants to train to be an actor would be better applying for actor training courses; many university courses are about studying drama in a wider context and would be frustrating for those who want specialist professional training (and have perhaps applied to academic university courses because their parents want them to).

WHAT DOES A GOOD PERSONAL STATEMENT LOOK LIKE?

Example of a good personal statement

I wish to study theatre/performance at university due to the passion I have for drama. What evokes this passion is the unique way drama allows for the exploration of the human condition, its history, its philosophies and beliefs and emotions therein. My enthusiasm has developed through a practical investigation of Miller, Fo, Shakespeare, Brecht and, more recently, Artaud and Grotowski. My understanding of theatre has been greatly enhanced by my English literature A level studies, through which I have broadened my knowledge of theatre history and revolutionary playwrights such as Marlowe. My understanding of photography has helped me to be creative and expressive in my work and to use imagery effectively. This has aided my study of drama, particularly in devised work. At university I desire to continue to learn, explore and further develop my performance skills and my understanding of the world of theatre.

I have aspirations to teach drama or to work professionally in theatre, perhaps by setting up a Theatre in Education company. In the light of this I have applied for a nine-month placement in Tanzania teaching English and drama in African schools. I feel participating in such a scheme will help me to mature further and develop communication skills and subject knowledge. I am a very self-motivated person who enjoys getting involved in extra-curricular activities. For example, in November I played Ophelia in the school production of 'Hamlet'. During this process I gained a greater appreciation of how the theatre works and how much effort goes into putting on a show. This understanding was further developed in April when I was given the role of deputy stage manager in a school production of the 'Threepenny Opera'. I am also a member of the school chamber choir and jazz choir.

✓ This statement shows someone who can think about the importance of drama within a wider context; the candidate is able to think about some of the functions of drama and also how their other A levels have broadened their understanding. The gap-year activities are pertinent to the subject and challenging. The candidate's interest in drama goes beyond acting or self-interest: the lead female role in 'Hamlet' provided a chance to think more about production aspects. The candidate shows that social activities have developed a sense of group membership, and that a drama course at a university is the right place for them to explore their subject.

 TOP TIPS

1 Indicate that you are aware that drama and theatre studies at university tend to combine the academic study of theatre with performance skills. Some courses place very little emphasis on performance. You need to express clearly that you understand the distinction between performance arts and theatre studies and make it clear that you believe that this is right for you

2 Illustrate your experience of performance with reference to live acts you have seen and how they have extended your knowledge of the subject

3 Talk about the skills you have learnt from your study of drama and theatre studies thus far

4 Emphasise the fact that you are personally motivated and willing to work hard and independently to achieve your goals

5 Detail the non-academic interests you have, especially if they involve working in an environment that promotes personal leadership and the need to overcome challenges without direct adult control, for instance the Duke of Edinburgh Award

 THINGS TO AVOID

1 Poorly constructed sentences with no clear direction or purpose

2 Spelling, grammar and punctuation errors

3 A statement that indicates that you have little understanding of the demands of the course. You need to demonstrate an awareness of the distinction between acting courses and drama/theatre studies

4 Making any claims that you would struggle to defend if called to interview or audition. This means no bare-faced lies or blatant plagiarism of statements that you might find on the internet. Be yourself!

RECOMMENDED READING AND WEBSITES

- Emma Govan, Helen Nicholson and Katie Normington, *Making a Performance: Devising Histories and Contemporary Practices,* Routledge, 2007
- Alison Hodge, *Actor Training*, Routledge, 2010
- Richard McCaw, *Bakhtin and Theatre: Dialogues with Stanislavsky, Meyerhold and Grotowski*, Routledge, 2015
- Dan Rebellato (ed.), *Modern British Playwriting 2000–2009: Voices, Documents, New Interpretations*, Methuen, 2013
- Arts Council England: www.artscouncil.org.uk
- Drama UK: www.dramauk.co.uk

I am grateful for the support of Royal Holloway, University of London (www.royalholloway.ac.uk/dramaandtheatre) in the preparation of this profile. Other highly rated courses include those at the University of East Anglia, the Guildhall School of Music and Drama, Queen Mary University of London and the Royal Central School of Speech and Drama, University of London.

ENGINEERING (CIVIL)

This academic profile was written using information provided by an admissions tutor at the University of Southampton and focuses on civil engineering as a single honours discipline. Engineering as a discipline at university is varied in its focus. Courses on offer include mechanical, aeronautical, structural, electrical and civil engineering. Each deal with a different aspect of human engineering needs and will require different skills, academic qualifications and interests. The information here is useful to all applicants, but some of the advice is pertinent to Southampton in particular.

SUBJECT OVERVIEW

Civil engineering applies science, mathematics, design and creativity to solve problems of critical importance to society, across construction, maintenance and management of infrastructure. We tend to take for granted the buildings we live and work in, the roads, railways and airports that allow us to travel, and the water that we use. It is professional civil engineers who make all this possible, and who are called on to find solutions to the major challenges facing the world in the future, such as the effects of climate change and sea-level rise, finding sustainable sources of energy and dealing with congestion.

These degree courses provide excellent preparation, in terms of knowledge and understanding and key transferable skills, for a career in civil engineering. Many courses are fully accredited by the Institution of Civil Engineers and the Institution of Structural Engineers, providing the first stage in a recognised career path to Chartered or Incorporated Engineer status. Employment prospects are excellent.

WHAT SKILLS OR ATTRIBUTES DO ADMISSIONS TUTORS LOOK FOR IN A GOOD APPLICANT?

The essential academic skills we look for are numeracy, problem-solving ability and logical thinking. Most entry requirements therefore include A level Mathematics and a science, or equivalent qualifications. Some top schools expect an A* in maths or physics A level. We also look for good communication skills in our students, both written and verbal. Other positive attributes are information technology skills, a practical hands-on attitude to situations, and design flair and creativity, particularly for the civil engineering with architecture course.

Where at all possible, any evidence of work experience in an engineering environment should be promoted. It need not be long or high powered, but it will show a genuine interest in this vocation. One good taster course is the well respected Headstart course.

Important personal qualities for a professional engineer are team-working skills and leadership ability, evidence of the potential for which we look for in candidates' personal statements where they describe sporting activities, clubs, societies, hobbies, voluntary activities or business games in which they have been actively involved.

WHAT DOES A GOOD PERSONAL STATEMENT LOOK LIKE?

Explain why you wish to pursue the particular line of study: here we would expect to see some brief background on why you wish to pursue a career in civil engineering. This could be related to a family link, for example working in the family's construction business, or other experiences, for instance seeing structures while on holiday, articles in books/journals/ the engineering press, work experience.

Describe the efforts you have already made to further your knowledge and understanding in the area: good applications always describe what steps the candidate has taken to find out more about the subject area. This is best done through practical experience in the form of work-experience placements with engineering firms, attending guest lectures or participating in an Engineering Headstart course at a university. You should briefly describe what you got out of the experience and how it has influenced you to apply for the course.

Describe other attributes that demonstrate your wider 'generic' skill-set: describe any relevant work experience you have had and how it has improved your communication, negotiation and team-building skills, for example, care in the community, shop work, engineering placements. Sporting achievements, clubs and society memberships, vocational qualifications and particularly any positions of responsibility taken within those areas should be highlighted, for example being a member of a football team or the Duke of Edinburgh Award. Any charity work can also be mentioned.

Link your generic skill-set to the needs of your chosen course: a good personal statement will go that step further and state how the skills learnt through your generic skills will benefit you during your course, for instance, leadership or team-working skills gained through a part-time job or while on a charity bike ride could help in undergraduate group projects or on a work placement.

 TOP TIPS

1 Present all your qualifications clearly and accurately

2 Write a succinct and clear personal statement, with a clear direction and flow from one point to another. Keep it concise and precise, promoting your skills in a compelling and interesting way

3 Demonstrate your understanding of what engineering is about, preferably drawing on examples of engineering that you have read about or personally experienced

4 Demonstrate that you are interested in applying maths and science to real problems – mention the fact that you enjoy puzzles, mental arithmetic and designing

5 Demonstrate in your personal statement activities that you have taken part in that show team-working and leadership skills

 THINGS TO AVOID

1 Ambiguous or missing information

2 Spelling or grammatical errors

3 Thinking that engineering is about fixing things such as washing machines or cars

4 Saying that you can't wait to move away from anything involving maths and science

5 Saying that your favourite hobby is going out with friends or watching the television – this is too often repeated and appears lazy and ill-prepared

RECOMMENDED READING AND WEBSITES

- James Burnett, *Getting into Engineering Courses*, Trotman Education, 2015
- Etrust: www.etrust.org.uk/headstart-inspire-ris – the website of the excellent taster courses in engineering and science. Well worth looking at if you have the time and inclination
- New Civil Engineer: www.newcivilengineer.com
- Construction News: www.constructionnews.co.uk
- Institution of Civil Engineers: www.ice.org.uk
- Engineering Council UK: www.engc.org.uk
- Institution of Engineering and Technology: www.theiet.org

I am grateful to the University of Southampton (www.southampton.ac.uk/engineering) for its support in the preparation of this profile. Other highly rated courses can be found at the universities of Sheffield, Imperial College, Edinburgh, Nottingham and Dundee.

ENGLISH

This academic profile was written using information provided by admissions tutors at Royal Holloway, King's College, Queen Mary (QMUL), all three part of the University of London. The information is useful to all applicants, but some of the advice is pertinent to Royal Holloway, King's College and Queen Mary in particular.

SUBJECT OVERVIEW

English is a versatile and interesting subject, characterised by the rigorous critical study of literature and language. It is concerned with the production, reception and interpretation of written texts, and with the literary and expressive potential of the English language. The study of English demands a constant commitment to improving your reading and writing skills. It develops a flexible and responsive openness of mind and advanced skills in argument, and encourages you to think critically for yourself about literature and life.

In the first year most students take a common set of courses that introduces them to some of the major areas of literary study and provides them with a historical understanding of literature that stretches back as far as the medieval period. This gives students the basis to progress to more advanced, specialised study of particular areas.

In the second and third years, students are able to choose from a number of optional courses as wide ranging as science fiction to Afro-American literature.

It is vital to research each department carefully and find out what it expects from you. If you love American literature, then do not apply to a department with no particular interest in that genre. This lazy approach will often lead to rejection in what is a very competitive application process. Take your time to choose the courses carefully and do not be swayed by the 'name' of the university.

A degree in English trains the mind and feeds the imagination; it provides a range of transferable skills, including oral and written presentation skills.

WHAT SKILLS OR ATTRIBUTES DO ADMISSIONS TUTORS LOOK FOR IN A GOOD APPLICANT?

Admissions tutors will always consider the level of attainment in GCSEs and predicted grades for A levels first of all. Many English courses now demand very high grades, simply due to supply and demand. It is not at all uncommon for candidates to be made offers of AAB or higher. Equally, it is not unusual for candidates to be rejected from one or more of their preferred universities. However, it is also possible to get into English courses with lower grades. Do your research carefully!

Many course admissions tutors take into account the GCSE profiles of candidates. They look for evidence of consistent academic performance across a range of subjects.

In addition to English A level, a good department will look for academic ability across a range of other subjects. It is important that candidates choose subjects in which they have a genuine interest, rather than taking them for strategic purposes. Successful applicants in recent years have studied subjects such as history, French, German, philosophy, film studies, politics, psychology and maths.

The personal statement and school reference are then read for any signs that there is a genuine interest in English literature. Tutors would hope to see indications of long-standing enjoyment, and an understanding that English at university will not be like three more years of A level English, but will be more demanding and unpredictable. We want to see evidence of wide reading and an appreciation of different literary genres.

Good applicants demonstrate excellent academic potential and enthusiasm for further study. They show both good time-management skills, necessary for independent study, and team-work skills, which are needed for seminar participation and group project work.

WHAT DOES A GOOD PERSONAL STATEMENT LOOK LIKE?

A good personal statement introduces your real passions and personality. Just as every student is different, so every statement should be different. However, successful statements will demonstrate a sincere love of literature that goes beyond the set texts at school. Cultural interests, widely defined, should appear such as theatre-going, gallery-visiting, films and music (if applicable).

Example from a good personal statement

> **During August, I volunteered to work as a literacy support assistant at my local library.**

✓ This is an example of real commitment to literature. The applicant saw reading as something of such utility and social value that she was helping others to begin.

Good statements also make it clear that the candidate wants to study literature and is interested in the kind of programme offered at a particular university.

QMUL stresses the importance of the personal statement, which will help to determine whether an applicant will be offered an interview. According to Dr Reid, a senior admissions tutor, your statement should illustrate dedication and enthusiasm to the subject area. He looks in particular for:

❝ an indication of intellectual and cultural interests, along with evidence of commitment to the subject area, and liveliness and independence of mind.**❞**

He also makes the point that for a department that interviews applicants, an effective personal statement is especially important because, more often than not,

❝ We use this part of the UCAS application as a starting point for discussion during the academic interview.**❞**

Dr Cornelia Cook, head of admissions for English, says that they are looking for 'evidence of wide and engaged reading' and, ultimately, a real commitment to the subject. And finally, if you do not want to be humiliated at interview (and not many applicants do), you need to be prepared to discuss anything mentioned in your personal statement, including any texts. This could prove tricky if you have exaggerated your achievements and/or fabricated hobbies to make yourself sound more interesting.

 TOP TIPS

1 The personal statement is an important discriminatory tool and therefore it should be prepared with care and attention to detail

2 It is preferable to devote one or two sentences to single examples than simply to list authors or titles. While space on the form is limited, admissions staff look for candidates who formulate their interests in as explanatory a way as possible

3 Admissions tutors look for clear evidence of liveliness and independence of mind

4 Clearly express the skills that you have learnt from the study of English and other subjects to A level or their equivalent

5 Tell the tutor about the extra-curricular pursuits you enjoy, but avoid just listing them. Concentrate on one or two activities that you feel particularly passionate about, and then tell them why and what you have learnt from the pursuit of these activities

6 Read as widely as possible, in particular other works by the authors you are studying, beyond the set texts. Experiencing performances of classic theatre, such as Shakespeare, or opera, would be beneficial

 THINGS TO AVOID

1 Poor spelling, punctuation, grammar and sentence construction. This is English, after all!

2 Failing to express your passion for English and not reinforcing it with examples that go beyond the remit of your A level course

3 Exaggerating your achievements and/or making up hobbies to make you sound more interesting – if you do not want to be humiliated at interview, you need to be prepared to discuss anything mentioned in your personal statement, including any texts

4 Plagiarism in any form

5 Applying for a course where the department clearly will not meet your interests as expressed in the statement

6 Avoid textbook-style generalisations. Try to express yourself in an intelligent but personal way

RECOMMENDED READING AND WEBSITES

- Explore some of the major works of pre-20th century literature – novelists such as Henry Fielding, Jane Austen, George Eliot, Charles Dickens; poets such as Donne, Wordsworth, Coleridge and Keats.

I am grateful to the English departments at Queen Mary University of London (www.english. qmul.ac.uk), King's College London (www.kcl.ac.uk/artshums/depts/english) and Royal Holloway, University of London (www.royalholloway.ac.uk/english) for their support in compiling this profile. Other highly rated courses include those at the universities of Oxford, Cambridge, Durham, Glasgow and Leeds.

ENVIRONMENTAL SCIENCE

This profile was written using information provided by an admissions tutor at the University of Southampton. Environmental science as a discipline is offered in a variety of different guises. These include single honours courses, environmental earth sciences, geophysical sciences and environmental geography. An increasing number of universities also now offer this as a joint honours degree with business management. This reflects its growing importance in the commercial world.

Each course relates to a different aspect of this branch of science and will require different skills, academic qualifications and interests. The information here is useful to all applicants, but some of the advice is pertinent to Southampton in particular.

SUBJECT OVERVIEW

Environmental scientists work in the public and private sectors to address the major and pressing issues facing human beings and the world we live in. As such, they are at the sharp end of dealing with many of the challenges that we face in the natural world. One has only to think of the impact that flooding had in late 2015 to see that their role is growing in national significance. Such problems have become regular headline news items over the last few years and include climate change, tsunamis, deforestation, pollution, destruction of wildlife, earthquakes and genetically modified organisms (GMOs).

Environmental science allows students to study for an interdisciplinary degree, cutting across the boundaries between traditional science subjects like biology, chemistry, geography, geology and oceanography, and usually with a large practical and field-based element. The skills are transferable and we find that students leave to work in large corporations such as BP, Atkins or Network Rail, or non-governmental organisations and charities, including overseas aid work. A good number are employed by the civil service in the Environment Agency.

Most degrees are modular, with a series of modules taken each year, building annually to increase the specialisation and complexity. Students often take a residential field course in year 1 to develop practical skills and can take a further residential field course in year 3, which is more student-led, involving extensive field data collection and reporting.

Note too, that many courses now link up with other disciplines such as geography, economics, business management or the natural sciences.

WHAT SKILLS OR ATTRIBUTES DO ADMISSIONS TUTORS LOOK FOR IN A GOOD APPLICANT?

Academic skills include communication (oral and written), team skills, numeracy, and some evidence of scientific practical skill is normally preferred. There are a wide range of different entry standards, from AAB at the top end to BCC at the lower end.

Most candidates who are offered places will have studied a science to A level (biology or chemistry) together with maybe maths, geography or economics.

Non-academic qualities include independence, commitment and resilience. As much of the time you work in teams, admissions tutors will look for this on the personal statement; have you led teams, worked in a team or presented to an audience?

WHAT DOES A GOOD PERSONAL STATEMENT LOOK LIKE?

Demonstrate your knowledge and enthusiasm: say why you really want to do this degree, what has inspired you and why. If you have been involved in any relevant activities, through school or college, or perhaps through voluntary work, you should tell us about that, too. We like to hear about fieldwork you have completed – where you went, what you did and what you learnt. What skills did you acquire and how might they help you at university?

Do tell admissions tutors about other things as well. If you are interested in sport or music that's fine, and achievement in non-academic areas can impress and show you are a good all-rounder. But focus mainly on your interest in the degree and why this is what you want to do, including any aspirations for your future career.

We want to see too an awareness of current media interest in this discipline and perhaps evidence that you have a career interest – this is not vital but will help.

Example of a good personal statement

> The environment is something I have always been passionate about. From an early age I have watched wildlife in our garden, observing the annual cycles of life. At the same time I have always been committed to taking positive steps to help our environment – getting my parents to recycle their newspapers and switching to low-energy light bulbs when I was still at primary school. Since then my knowledge has expanded and my commitment has grown. I was chairman of a student group that recently helped my school to gain EcoSchool status, and I was co-ordinator of our conservation group, creating a nature trail in the school grounds and working as volunteers on local nature reserves. I am also a member of my local Friends of the Earth group, and have been actively involved in their recent campaigns about overfishing, including attending a large demonstration in London.

✓ This demonstrates long-term commitment to issues relevant to the degree.

> My inspiration has increasingly come from my studies and the reading I have done to support them. I have immersed myself in the works of Aldo Leopold such as 'Sand County Almanac' – although these were written in the first half of the last century the lessons about prudent use of our world's resources apply more than ever today.

✓ Good evidence of academic commitment and knowledge, well written.

> Inspired by work such as that, and by the global leadership of Al Gore and the Intergovernmental Panel on Climate Change, I now want to study for a degree that will both challenge me intellectually and lead to a worthwhile and rewarding career. I chose my A levels in chemistry, geography and biology with an environmental sciences degree in mind. I enjoy practical work, both in the laboratory and in the field, and put them to good use in a work placement last summer in the Environment Agency's laboratories, analysing water quality.

✓ Relevant to this type of course, and an indication of skills.

> Our field trip to Belize changed my life – the wealth of environmental riches in Latin America is truly astounding – with coral reefs, rainforests and wildlife, as well as remarkable local cultures – but the threats they may face in future years from the activities of humans are alarming.

✓ Good example, nicely summarised.

> I hope one day to work in research into managing conservation areas in developing countries, and have taken Spanish AS this year to help develop some useful language skills.

✓ Shows forward planning, strategic thinking and some ambitious career aspirations.

Example of a poor personal statement

> I think an environmental sciences degree would be really good for me to study. It will be really interesting to find out more about our world.

✗ No depth here.

> I became interested in this when I realised that I wasn't going to get good enough grades to study to be a vet at university.

✗ Not a good admission to make.

> I have since noticed how much things like climate change are on the TV news.

✗ Not specific enough.

> I have always been interested in animals, and keep reptiles at home, and would like to learn more about them and how they behave.

✗ So, does he still want to be a vet, really?

> I play guitar for an indie rock band called Armageddon Death Bomb, which I started with some friends at school. We have worked really hard, and practise most days, which can make it difficult to keep up with school work. We are hoping to play at some festivals this summer and if we do well I might take a gap year to see if we can be successful.

✗ This shows commitment, but not to anything academic or relevant to the degree.

 TOP TIPS

1 In the opening paragraph, let the tutor know why it is that you have been drawn towards the subject and what evidence you can provide that indicates you have an understanding of the demands of the course

 THINGS TO AVOID

1 Spelling and punctuation mistakes – get your statement proofread carefully

2 Lies or claims that you would struggle to defend in an interview

2 Let them know about any extended reading or fieldwork opportunities that you might have had or any extra-curricular interests that pertain to the degree specifically, for example, conservation projects or recycling initiatives

3 Promote your existing skills in science-based subjects and other related subjects such as geography – what skills you have acquired and what your particular strengths are

4 Show that you are aware of the current issues that relate to the subject and that you read quality journalism and literature. Mention any particular area of the subject that especially interests you and explain why

5 Give some indication that you are an independent learner with the personal initiative required to thrive in this environment

6 Write about your interests beyond school and college – focus too on any relevant experience that might show your commitment to the course. Show things that emphasise your leadership and team skills. Have you had to overcome any difficulties?

3 Copying someone else's statement – we want to get to know you, not them!

4 Too much emphasis on interests that are irrelevant to your chosen course

5 Not using up the full amount of space – this leaves a bad impression unless the rest of the statement is outstanding

6 Bland lists of achievements that do not help your case. Ask yourself – why is this relevant?

 # RECOMMENDED READING AND WEBSITES

- Works by authors such as Richard Dawkins, Steve Jones, James Lovelock, Aldo Leopold, Rachel Carson are good for general reading around the subject
- A good daily newspaper, to ensure that you are aware of current issues facing the discipline
- *New Scientist*: www.newscientist.com
- Environment Agency: www.gov.uk/government/organisations/environment-agency
- Institution of Environmental Sciences: www.the-ies.org

I am grateful to the Environmental Science department at the University of Southampton (www.southampton.ac.uk/engineering/what_we_do/environmental_science.page) for its support in compiling this profile. Other highly rated courses include those at the universities of Leicester, Manchester, Imperial College and East Anglia.

FINE ART AND ART FOUNDATION

This academic profile was written using information provided by an admissions tutor from the University of Dundee (which includes Duncan of Jordanstone College of Art & Design). The information in this profile is useful to all applicants, but please be aware that some of the advice is pertinent to that department in particular.

SUBJECT OVERVIEW

Students wishing to study fine art at university normally undertake a one-year Foundation programme first that equips them to apply for a three-year BA honours degree in Fine Art. In Scotland students enter a four-year degree programme in art or design, the first year of which is normally a diagnostic General Foundation in Art and Design.

The first aim of a Foundation course is the development of your ability, skill and critical faculties by means of thoughtful study and practical artwork. An awareness of the broad nature of art and design underlies the teaching of the course. The process of acquiring sound basic skills includes consideration of creativity, aesthetics, visual awareness and analytical and critical faculties. Knowledge and a sense and understanding of the history, theory and practice of art and design are cultivated, allowing you to place yourself, your work and aspirations in context.

The second aim is to help you decide, from the varied modules undertaken, your choice of degree study for the subsequent three years. The make-up of the modules has been carefully devised to enable you to gain a broad experience, awareness and level of skill allied to art and design practices.

Parallel to this is the contribution that the overall dynamic of the course, as a learning experience, makes to the progressive development of your sense of connection to a specific area of subject specialism.

These twin aims are achieved through students working alongside each other in studios on projects led by academic staff.

During their Foundation year, students will apply to the degree specialism of their choice. This will involve preparing an application and accompanying portfolio. Students may be invited for an interview. The selection process will identify students who will benefit from a fine art education. The aims of a fine art programme include:

- to offer students the opportunity to develop their potential as independent artists in a multidisciplinary culture and an atmosphere of creative innovation and endeavour
- to produce graduates who are confident in their chosen areas of practice, who have developed visual imagination and awareness, and have acquired many personal and interpersonal, professional, transferable and research skills
- to develop the *students'* understanding of the artistic, historical, theoretical and cultural context which informs and shapes practice
- to develop the students' critical and self-critical capacities.

Students on fine art programmes may specialise in one particular discipline, such as sculpture, but increasingly students work across a range of visual disciplines in pursuit of the visualisation of their ideas. They will have opportunities to participate in study visits and to display their work in exhibitions. Most degree programmes will culminate in an annual public degree exhibition.

WHAT SKILLS OR ATTRIBUTES DO ADMISSIONS TUTORS LOOK FOR IN A GOOD APPLICANT?

Your portfolio will be considered to assess your enthusiasm, creativity, intellectual and practical skills in the practice of art and design. Consideration will be given to your potential for further development and progress in any of the fields of art and design that the college has to offer.

The selector(s) will also be looking for indications of your visual awareness, the range of your interests and experience and the level of your commitment to art and design. Your portfolio should include representative examples of work undertaken as part of a programme of study. The compilation of a portfolio should not be regarded as an end in itself but, rather, as one of the results of that study. It is the primary means by which you present yourself to the selector, so you should prepare it accordingly.

WHAT DOES A GOOD PERSONAL STATEMENT LOOK LIKE?

Your portfolio is the primary tool for the selection process, but your personal statement adds a valuable context. It should be imaginative and creative. You should demonstrate creativity and a desire to pursue a career in art. Admissions tutors are interested in hearing about school and extra-curricular activities, but only where they demonstrate in a broader context how they have helped to develop you as a person in relation to your artistic aspirations.

Examples from good personal statements

> Having been involved in and thoroughly enjoyed art and design during my years at school, culminating in advanced Higher Art and Design and portfolio this year, I am now sure that my chosen future career will be art related.

✓ This is a clear, unambiguous and honest opening sentence.

> It may seem unoriginal, but the arts have always been an important part of my life. I would describe myself as a creative person and am interested in the links between the visual arts and language. To quote artist Jackson Pollock, 'It is all a big game of construction – some with a brush, others choose a pen.'

✓ This opening shows a wider awareness of the cultural context of art. It also demonstrates an appreciation of the links between different aspects of the creative arts.

> Summer of 2014 enabled me to address my future and determine my choice of study. It was during that time that I realised that my interests in both art and computer graphics could be combined. I was very lucky to get the opportunity to work with a games company as a games tester. I gained invaluable experience in learning how the business side of the industry worked as well as the creative process.
>
> During my fifth year at school I found the Higher Art course enjoyably challenging. I had to work to strict deadlines on two units – jewellery design producing a piece inspired by the Botanic Gardens, and portraiture, which involved painting a self-portrait. I also learnt about several painters from different movements. During that year I also attended a summer school at a local college and went on to join a life-drawing class and portfolio-building class.

✓ These two examples demonstrate the initiative and commitment shown through a wider involvement with art-related studies beyond the school or further education curriculum.

> Outside of college I have a part-time job in Asda where I interact with many different types of people, colleagues and customers. This job has helped me improve my communication skills in 'day to day' life and to become more confident. At school I enjoyed the challenge of being the

chair of a school committee that organised events to raise money for charity both in and outside school. For example, we raised funds for Red Nose Day and I was involved in making posters to raise awareness as well as making a short film that was shown to various year groups to encourage fellow pupils and staff to give money.

✓ An individual demonstrating how they invest their creative abilities in a wider context.

I was also a prefect, a role from which I learnt better timekeeping and became more mature and responsible. I also developed other skills during my time in sixth year through helping a first year academically and socially as part of the buddying system. Not only did I enjoy this but I learnt to listen and be patient and to be aware of how other people use situations.

✓ This is an acknowledgement of the collective responsibility and contribution that can be made in a community. It also displays an awareness of the personal attributes acquired through taking on roles of responsibility

I decided I wanted to study art so I looked at various course options. I had heard that particular courses were excellent so I took the opportunity to go to their open days. I was particularly attracted by the course at ... and the Foundation year seemed a good way to discover which area of art would suit me, however, at present I feel I would like to pursue sculpture.

✓ Shows that the applicant has seriously researched the options available and made a considered choice of application.

The following statement stood out from the crowd – it was the second year that the student had applied and this statement played a strong supporting role to her portfolio in the decision to offer her a place. She is now studying graphic design.

Me? I love: unexpected snow, my friends, surprises, gifts, noodles, music, computing, socialising, writing, spontaneity, the smell of petrol/bleach/vanilla, strawberry jam, old photographs, my family, meddling, new socks, guitars, being random, driving through puddles, heavy rain, apple juice, gigs, camping, tartan mini skirts with hoodies and so much more, but above all else I love art. I know that may seem like one heck of a generalisation, but it's true. I love everything from paintings that seem like photographs (Michelangelo) to ones that verge on the obscure (Francis Bacon), sketches that must have taken hours (Da Vinci) to comic strips (John Allison), to graffiti (Banksy), to elaborate sculptures (Mark Quinn) and everything in between!

This year I have been indulging and further extending my love for all things arty by attending Dundee College on a full-time portfolio course. Through this I feel that I have greatly enhanced my skills and knowledge in drawing, design and painting. In general, I enjoy the expressive subjects more than design, but on the whole I enjoy the whole course, with my favourite class changing every week! I also feel that my social and interpersonal skills have developed as I have made many new friends and had the chance to meet people whom I otherwise would have not.

In particular, my life drawing has come on tremendously as I currently attend a night course at college. I am thoroughly enjoying it as I never had the chance to do it at school and I feel it helps, not just with my life drawing, but also other aspects of the subject. I also plan to start a night class on using Dreamweaver later in the year as I am particularly interested in the areas of graphic design and the internet.

Going to Dundee College has meant that I have had to give up my cleaning job as the hours were incompatible as I have to travel by train every day and I arrive home late at night, but it's all been worthwhile.

Outside of college I enjoy going to various art galleries to look at what is happening in the art world and to see different exhibitions. I feel that it is important to have an interest in a wide variety of art as all aspects of it overlap and tie in with each other, so a technique used in fine art may in fact help with something in design. This way I feel that I am broadening the range of techniques and skills I have for the future.

Although the workload has been demanding this year I have found it a welcome change to school, where I was vice captain of my house and had to perform various duties such as organising house events and maintaining the house noticeboard (a harder task than it sounds when you get no help from your captain!). I was also in charge of the lockers, which meant I had to make sure they were properly maintained and distributed. All the duties I had to perform in secondary school have helped make me become more organised and more reliable. I also now know that I am capable of working not just in a team but I can also work on my own competently.

Overall I feel that I am ready to further my education by attending university, where I hope to continue to enjoy the subject as much as I have done in the past and to carry on learning and adding to my artistic abilities. I believe that I am a conscientious, organised and self-motivated person who will cope well with the demands of university life. Irrespective of my long-term career path, I am confident that my all-round abilities would serve me well in an art course. I am keen to broaden my horizons in an academic, social and personal sense and feel that university study will provide many opportunities for development.

Examples from poor personal statements

It was clear to me from a very young age that art was my great passion, not only because I was told I was talented, but because I enjoyed everything about it. I was never happier than when spending all my hours in the school art department.

✗ This opening paragraph is a cliché – both in language and sentiment.

As a child I was deeply unhappy if I didn't have my crayons with me. In my spare time I like to read, sketch or paint. I get a real thrill and am inspired by producing a completely original piece of work. This feeling drives me to achieve my ambition at a much higher level.

✗ This comes across as being naïve. It reads as if this is a hobby rather than a serious commitment.

I was elected school prefect in my final year and was involved in an anti-bullying initiative. I also attend a local church and teach in the Sunday School. For several years I attended karate lessons. At present I am in my second year of being a prefect at school, which is a very responsible position. I study a lot in my free time as well as working part time doing clerical work in a local office. In school I was asked by the learning support unit to assist students with learning difficulties with their school work.

✗ This is just a list of achievements with no acknowledgement of the skills the writer has developed through these activities.

 TOP TIPS

1 Your portfolio is the primary tool for the selection process, but your personal statement adds a valuable context – it should be imaginative and creative

2 Get someone else to read over your statement before you send it. It is very easy to overlook grammatical and spelling errors, lack of punctuation, repetition and omitting vital information

3 Emphasise your love of art and the artistic process – convey this passion in a way that is compelling and unusual

4 Draw on what influences you now and any artist or artistic genre you find compelling

 THINGS TO AVOID

1 Copying examples of personal statements you find on the web – you should use them as a only guideline. They are easy to spot and result in statements that do not show the individuality that selectors are looking for

2 Using clichés and overtly 'arty' language

3 Implying that art is a hobby, not an intellectual passion

4 Telling lies and near-truths that can be exposed at interview

---

 RECOMMENDED READING AND WEBSITES

- James Burnett, *Getting into Art and Design Courses*, Trotman Education, 2016
- Alan Pipes, *Foundations of Art and Design*, Laurence King Publishing, 2008
- Arts Council England: www.artscouncil.org.uk
- Arts Council Northern Ireland: www.artscouncil-ni.org
- Arts Council Wales: www.artswales.org.uk
- Scottish Arts Council: www.scottisharts.org.uk
- a-n The Artists Information Company: www.a-n.co.uk

I am grateful for the support of Duncan of Jordanstone College of Art & Design (www.dundee. ac.uk/djcad) in compiling this profile. Other highly rated courses can be found at colleges such as Slade, Camberwell, Central School, Glasgow and Goldsmiths.

GEOGRAPHY

This academic profile was written using information provided by an admissions tutor at Royal Holloway, University of London. The information in this profile is useful to all applicants, but some of the advice is pertinent to that department in particular.

SUBJECT OVERVIEW

Geography is a diverse and exciting subject, which allows students to explore and understand the key environmental, economic, social and political challenges we face in the modern world. Many departments, including Royal Holloway, offer the BA, BSc and BA Human Geography course. All are different, with different emphasis and entry expectations. It is safe to say, though, that a BSc course is more likely to include a greater proportion of physical geography and may have a science A level entry requirement. Do your research!

Geography degrees at Royal Holloway are flexible, allowing you to explore the broad range of geographical topics, or to focus on particular areas of interest. This is something that ought to be typical of all good courses.

Learning about the environment, sustainable development, climate change, globalisation and other issues that affect our lives is an essential part of modern geography. The subject is unique in providing a bridge between the social sciences, with their understanding of the dynamics of societies, cultures and behaviour, and the environmental sciences, with their understanding of physical landscapes and the dynamics of environmental processes. The interaction between people and the environment lies at the heart of the discipline and is essential to contemporary understanding of today's global problems.

By studying such a broad subject, students obtain a range of learning experiences and skills that make geography graduates highly attractive to future employers.

The Royal Geographical Society states that on completion of your degree you will have gained many skills in preparation for work. These will be integral to your training, and to your employability, and should include:

- intellectual skills, such as critically evaluating theories and judging evidence to make informed decisions and to develop reasoned arguments

- geography-specific skills, such as undertaking a piece of research using a range of technical methods for the collection and analysis of spatial and environmental data, and undertaking fieldwork
- key transferable skills in communication, presentation, debate, numerical analysis, team-work, problem solving, report and essay writing and many IT skills
- personal attributes, such as time management, development of responsibility, coping with uncertainty, self-reflection, motivation, flexibility and creativity.

Assessment of courses is through written examinations and/or coursework. The amount will vary year on year and between departments.

Coursework is designed to assess a range of skills, with typical methods including essays, subject reviews, laboratory reports, oral and poster presentations, fieldwork reports and the final year dissertation.

On a year-by-year basis, the balance between coursework and examinations could reasonably be expected to be as follows:

First year
Four exams, oral and poster presentations plus a report linked to the Spain field trip; field and laboratory reports, small-group tutorial work. Overall weighting is 50%:50% coursework to exams.

Second year
Three option courses each with 50% coursework and 50% exam; field and laboratory reports. Overall weighting is approximately 63%:37% coursework to exams.

Third year
Dissertation; option courses and a 60%:40% bias towards written exams.

WHAT SKILLS OR ATTRIBUTES DO ADMISSIONS TUTORS LOOK FOR IN A GOOD APPLICANT?

We are looking for individuals who are passionate about geography and curious about the world in which we live. It is important that this interest goes beyond the confines of the curriculum and classroom, for example through attending outside lectures or reading geography-related books or magazines. Your should be able to see how geography helps to explain human and environmental processes in everyday life. Your statement must include evidence of this passion, with an awareness of how the subject impacts on the wider world. What books or journals have you read to support this interest? What fieldwork have you done and what did you learn? What parts of the geography you have studied so far excite you and how have they motivated you to read geography at university?

Studying at university requires students to be self-motivated and independent. How can you show that in your application? Think about that.

Applicants need to have developed good communication skills that allow them to present information effectively in both written and oral forms. They also need to have good ICT and data-analysis skills, and to be able to manage their time successfully and to work in groups.

Good applicants are well-rounded individuals who have interests beyond their school work. Activities such as sport, music and drama, as well as community work or paid employment, all involve skills development and will help you to meet the challenges of university study. Please do not just list the things you do – be choosy and think 'Why is this helpful or relevant?'

WHAT DOES A GOOD PERSONAL STATEMENT LOOK LIKE?

Example of a good personal statement

From an applicant who wants to study a physical geography course.

I have always been fascinated with geography and the way in which landforms are created. I enjoy both physical and human geography, but my main interests lie in the physical aspects. Pursuing geography to degree level has been a logical step for me. I want to develop my knowledge of geomorphological and environmental processes and, after graduation, find employment in a related field in either an academic or commercial environment.

My school field trip to Arran gave me the opportunity to investigate a very different landscape, and see the role of tectonic processes and glaciation in forming features such as sills and dykes, raised beaches and U-shaped valleys. I regularly attend Geographical Association lectures and particularly enjoyed a recent talk on coastal management in East Anglia. I also subscribe to 'Geography Review' magazine, which helps develop my understanding of geography.

My other A level subjects complement my interest in geography. For example, biology has helped me when studying ecosystems and maths has been important in the statistical analysis of fieldwork data. In all my A level courses, I have developed my skills in presenting information in written and oral form and using ICT.

For my work experience, I spent a week in the environmental department of the local council, focusing on their work related to the sustainable management of rivers and floodplains. With the increasing demand for housing in my local area, it is vital that planners consider flood risk when making decisions about urban development. I attended community consultation meetings as well as analysing maps showing high-risk floodplain locations. Such work demonstrates the practical contributions that geography can make in improving our lives.

I am passionate about sport and have played football for my school team for the past five years. Last year I was selected to play at county level and I hope to continue playing at university. Combining sport and school work requires good time management and organisation. Outside of school time I have a part-time job at my local supermarket. This has improved my self-confidence, team-work and communication skills.

I believe that I am a hard-working and motivated student, who can prioritise and deal with workloads and deadlines. I can use my initiative and remain open minded. I believe that university will allow me to become even more independent and will provide many opportunities to broaden my interests further. The chance to increase my knowledge in a subject that I enjoy immensely is extremely attractive.

The key aspects that make this a good personal statement are:

✓ A strong opening statement that shows why the applicant wants to study geography.

✓ They provide evidence that they understand what geography is about and what they have learnt from their study of geography so far. Bringing in some details about the landforms of Arran helps to support claims about being interested in landform formation.

✓ Including information about geography-related activities (going to Geographical Association lectures and reading *Geography Review*) demonstrates an interest and curiosity in the subject that goes beyond the classroom.

✓ The applicant shows an awareness of how geography intersects with other subjects and what skills they have developed in their A levels.

✓ There is recognition of how geography can be applied to real-world problems. This shows that they have thought about what geography is as a subject.

✓ Information is provided about interests and work experience, and what skills they have helped the applicant to develop.

✓ The final section sums up what personal qualities the applicant has that make them suitable to study geography at university.

✓ No spelling or grammar mistakes!

 TOP TIPS

1 Indicate that you understand what geography is about and that you are aware of the demands of the course

2 Show clearly any experiences that you have of coursework and fieldwork and what they taught you

3 Indicate an awareness of how geography intersects with other subjects and what skills you have gained from the study of other A levels

4 Provide evidence of your extra-curricular pursuits, particularly where these indicate leadership potential or personal initiative

 THINGS TO AVOID

1 Poor spelling, punctuation and grammar

2 Underselling your current skills

3 Indicating a poor understanding of the demands of the course, due to poor research – for instance, confusing physical and human geography

RECOMMENDED READING AND WEBSITES

- Paul Cloke, Philip Crang and Mark Goodwin (eds), *Introducing Human Geographies*, 3rd edition, Routledge, 2013
- Joseph Holden (ed.) *An Introduction to Physical Geography and the Environment*, 3rd edition, Pearson, 2012
- *Geography Review* magazine. Published four times a year by Philip Allan: www.hoddereducation.co.uk/geographyreviewextras
- The Royal Geographical Society with the Institute of British Geographers: www.rgs.org; www.rgs.org/OurWork/Study+Geography/Study+Geography
- Geographical Association: www.geography.org.uk

I am grateful for the support of Royal Holloway, University of London (www.royalholloway.ac.uk/geography/home.aspx) in the compiling of this profile. Other highly rated courses can be found at the universities of Cambridge, Oxford, Bristol, St Andrews and Edinburgh.

GEOLOGY

This academic profile was written by an admissions tutor at the University of Southampton. The information in this profile is useful to all applicants, but some of the advice is pertinent to Southampton in particular. Many geology departments are now part of bigger faculties; the one at Southampton is part of the Ocean and Earth Science Department. As such, there are many opportunities to study geology as a single honours subject or as a joint honours degree.

SUBJECT OVERVIEW

Geology is one of the most exciting, dynamic and relevant sciences in the world today. Geological investigations hold the key to many current global challenges. This includes understanding past climatic perturbation in order to predict future climate change, developing ways to discover new natural resources and exploit known ones responsibly, and understanding natural hazards and mitigating them.

Geology integrates many other scientific disciplines in the study of the nature, dynamics and evolution of the physical, chemical and biological processes operating on the Earth over the past four billion years – and even extends to studying other bodies in the solar system.

A degree in geology will enable you to study a wide spectrum of scientific disciplines and acquire subject-specific and transferable skills that are much sought after by employers. The continued demand for raw materials such as oil, gas and minerals ensures there will be a continued need for graduate geologists for many years to come. An undergraduate degree in geology will involve many diverse but integrated activities: lectures to provide theory and knowledge, laboratory practicals to teach fundamental analytical and practical skills, and fieldwork, both on one-day excursions and on residential courses in the UK and abroad, to provide hands-on training in geological field techniques and mapping.

All good courses will include instruction and practice in professional key skills such as report/essay writing, giving lectures and presentations and presenting papers and posters – all things you will be doing as a graduate scientist. All of this information will be provided in a coherent and progressive manner, and there will be a huge variety of different assessment methods, from written and practical exams to team-work projects, independent research, posters and oral presentations, all delivered in a way that is accessible and enjoyable to all.

Being taught by active researchers in their own field of expertise is always beneficial because research scientists can be counted on not only to be enthusiastic about their subject and to pass on their enthusiasm to you, but also to provide instruction on cutting-edge topics that form the current focus of international investigation.

You should expect to be challenged and have your abilities stretched throughout the duration of your degree, and should be able to demonstrate that you can apply what you have learnt in problem-based exercises.

Fieldwork should be a key element of your course and you should be taught how to use field equipment and how to collect, analyse and interpret a variety of different types of field data and samples.

All degree courses accredited by the Geological Society of London will offer an independent mapping project of some form, taking the form of several weeks' worth of field surveying somewhere in the world, usually in the summer vacation between the second and third years of study. Take care to choose the course that offers you the best fieldwork opportunities.

There will be support staff to guide and instruct you to successfully complete these specialised activities, but self-motivation and time-management skills are also essential!

Courses on offer range from BSc in Geology to MSc in Geology with a year abroad. Courses that offer a year abroad are very highly sought after. The grades to get in vary from university to university but are normally ABB to BCC for good institutions. Most will expect a science A level (chemistry being preferred) and perhaps geography.

WHAT SKILLS OR ATTRIBUTES DO ADMISSIONS TUTORS LOOK FOR IN A GOOD APPLICANT?

Applicants should display a drive and enthusiasm for, and an informed understanding of, the degree programme(s) for which they have applied, and should be able to demonstrate that they have thoroughly researched the subject area and have considered why they wish to undertake such a degree in the context of their future career development. Applicants will be expected to have ensured that their academic background and the examinations they are yet to take are acceptable, and that their qualifications will be of a sufficient level to ensure admission to the course of their choice.

Applicants should provide sufficient information in their personal statement to indicate that they not only appreciate the personal skills and abilities required for successful completion of an earth science degree, but that they can illustrate this appreciation with pertinent personal examples in the form of educationally based experience (for example, personal and team-based sporting or musical activities), extra-curricular or work experience. If an applicant can provide evidence or demonstrate well-developed time and personal management skills, English language, grammar and numerical skills, along with a degree of independence, these are all aspects of a candidate's character that will be of interest to admissions staff.

WHAT DOES A GOOD PERSONAL STATEMENT LOOK LIKE?

Your personal statement should provide an admissions tutor with sufficient information to convey not only that you have drive and enthusiasm for the degree programme(s) for which you are applying, but also that you have thoroughly researched the subject area and have considered why you wish to undertake such a degree in the context of your future career development. As a potential applicant you will be expected to tailor your personal statement to address your interest in the wider subject discipline and, perhaps, in specific areas of the discipline. To realise this you may choose to draw upon your own experiences in A level subjects, involvement in subject-related extra-curricular activities or work experience. Do emphasise any project work you have done at school and talk about this specifically. This part of the statement ought to comprise some 30–50% of the whole statement, and should be reflective and demonstrate self-awareness.

As all earth and marine science subject areas will have a practical, field-based component, you ought to highlight any such experience and skills which you already have, be they study-based or extra-curricular.

However, many of the personal skills and abilities required for successful completion of an earth or marine science degree can also be demonstrated by reference to other forms of education-based experience (for example, personal and individual/team-based sporting or musical activities), or work experience.

Avoid meaningless literary quotes or apparently deep, thoughtful insights about your chosen topic that you have picked off a website or invented – admission tutors have read most of them already!

Example of a good personal statement

While one child may have picked up a rock and skimmed it across the sea, my inquiring mind would not let me do this – I had to know more about that rock: where it came from, how it was formed. As a young child I was fascinated by rocks and earth materials around me – as I grew older, learning about plate tectonics and earthquakes through secondary school intrigued me further. I am currently studying biology and chemistry, both of which have a strong affiliation to geology and have provided me with additional scientific skills applicable to my geography course. I came to understand more about igneous, sedimentary and metamorphic rocks, permeable and impermeable rocks and the properties of materials such as chalk and clay, and I have recently attended a Geography Masterclass at the University of …, where aspects of environmental geography were discussed and developed. I subscribe to 'Geology Today', in which I have read articles such as 'From microscopic minerals to global climate change' by David J. Brown and Martin Lee. Articles of this kind have provided me with more in-depth views on the causes of climate change. I have recently conducted field trips to The Lizard in Cornwall, where one can stand up on the Moho, and up to the top of Mount Nephin in Ireland. It was in Ireland where I completed my pilot study, mapping a series of dykes inside a mainly metamorphic region. Earlier this year I went on fieldwork to Le Massif Central in France, where I completed my coursework of mapping and deducing the geological history of the area around Lac Chambon, and it was in France that I finally realised the true scale to which I am amazed by volcanoes, while stood at the top of Puie du Marie. On these trips I have gained valuable knowledge from the field and a first-hand understanding of geology. I especially enjoy the challenge of fieldwork, as I get the chance to explore new regions and broaden my ever expanding-horizons, making the most of what I can achieve: be it climbing a rock face to investigate a mineral vein, or contemplating a geological map. I'm a very 'outdoors' person and adverse weather doesn't bother me!

My desire to obtain a glimpse into what life is like as a geological researcher drove me to apply for a position on a five-week expedition to Disko Island, off the western coast of Greenland, this summer. While in Greenland we studied how glaciers had formed the valleys there, and mapped some of the geological features. The data we gathered about the movement of the snouts of the glaciers will be accessible to scientists around the world for research into climate change. This expedition not only allowed me to experience geological fieldwork further, but improved my motivation and determination and allowed me to develop as a person. The expedition also required me to raise over £4,500 in under a year, which I achieved through working part time, participating in a sponsored run and organising a first-aid course for local mountaineers.

I have been actively involved in several projects in school that I believe have provided me with the opportunities to mature as a young person. I am currently mentoring students in the year below me and helping them to achieve similar success. Last year I became a reading partner for younger students, which I feel greatly benefitted them as well as giving me valuable experience in working sympathetically with younger children. In my spare time I enjoy participating in sports, and am a qualified RYA Dinghy Instructor and later this year will be completing my Basic Expedition Leadership Award, which will allow me to run Duke of Edinburgh Award expeditions. I also enjoy supporting others, and was a prefect in the Lower Sixth and am currently on the Senior Prefect team at my school for Upper Sixth. My voluntary teaching at my sailing club is recognised by the Millennium Volunteer Scheme, where I have so far spent over 150 hours volunteering. These hobbies have developed my leadership skills and have pushed me to manage my time effectively, so that I can make the most of all the opportunities open to me. Furthermore, I have had the opportunity to meet a wide range of people and learn important skills in leadership and communication. I feel I have the maturity and enthusiasm to appreciate the academic opportunities offered at university and I am looking forward to participating in the activities that are available.

✓ This personal statement covers all of the subjects that admissions tutors in this subject area wish to read about.

✓ There is evidence of the candidate's enthusiasm for the degree subject for which they have applied, and the statement illustrates their in-depth understanding and appreciation of the specific areas of the discipline.

✓ The applicant provides ample indications of their drive and interest in the subject by having made strenuous efforts to accumulate subject-based practical extra-curricular experience (although we do not expect all applicants to offer such 'exotic' experience!).

✓ In later parts of the statement the applicant indicates very strong self-awareness of their own skills, abilities and limitations – and their willingness to push themselves in every aspect of their life, both academic and personal. This is invaluable information for someone trying to assess an applicant's aptitude for university-level studies.

 TOP TIPS

1 Although this is not directly related to the statement, please ensure your qualifications meet published admissions criteria for the particular degree course for which you are applying (you'd be amazed at the number of applications that get rejected due to applicants applying

 THINGS TO AVOID

1 Applying for courses without having checked you have the correct qualifications to offer

2 Poor spelling and use of grammar

3 If you are applying for several different but related subjects on your UCAS form, do no focus your personal

without the correct subjects or number of qualifications)

2 Provide honest and reflective comments about why you wish to study at university and what you want to achieve, as well as checking that your grammar and spelling are correct!

3 Describe and evaluate as fully as possible what you gained from the coursework and fieldwork you have already completed through your school or college

statement on one of these to the detriment of the others – admissions tutors see only the degree course you have applied for at their individual institution and they will not be impressed if your statement focuses on a different course at another institution

4 Trying to impress using literary quotes, or unlikely and apparently deeply thoughtful insights about your degree subject

RECOMMENDED READING AND WEBSITES

- Geologists' Association: www.geologists.org.uk
- British Geological Survey: www.bgs.ac.uk
- Cogent Skills: www.cogentskills.com

I am grateful to the Geology Department at the University of Southampton (www.southampton.ac.uk/oes/index.page) for its support in compiling this profile. Other highly rated courses include those at the universities of Bangor, Southampton and Aberdeen.

HISTORY

This academic profile was written using information provided by an admissions tutor at Royal Holloway, University of London. The information in this profile is useful to all applicants, but some of the advice is pertinent to that department in particular.

SUBJECT OVERVIEW

With global societies changing at a rapid pace, history has perhaps never been so relevant. The study of history concerns our understanding of what it was to be human in another place and at another time. Exploring what others have felt, thought and done in the past expands our self-awareness and our understanding of how we have come to be who we are, both as individuals and as members of a wider society.

Most good departments offer both single honours degrees (mostly BA) and joint honours degrees. Royal Holloway offers history with English, politics, ancient history, philosophy or modern languages. Many other options are out there, so look at them carefully.

Studying history sharpens your insights into the functioning of past societies, helping you to formulate a more critical awareness of current-day problems. In understanding past cultures and learning to respect the reasoned views of others, students learn the values of tolerance and acceptance of diversity, which are essential today. Furthermore, curiosity informs all historical enquiries and studying history encourages the application of skills of analysis, argument and critical thinking, which are all highly valued in the modern employment market. As a result, you will not only be highly employable, an important fact to note, but also have skills that are easily transferable.

Most good departments are also keen to hear from pupils from widening participation backgrounds. If you are the first in your family to attend university or have overcome hurdles to get to where you are now, do let us know.

WHAT SKILLS OR ATTRIBUTES DO ADMISSIONS TUTORS LOOK FOR IN A GOOD APPLICANT?

Most of all, admissions tutors are looking for enthusiasm for history; you need to want to steep yourself in the subject for three years. We are particularly looking for candidates who show that their enthusiasm goes far beyond the confines of the curriculum, for example by attending lectures, visiting historical sites and reading widely in history in their spare time.

Make sure that you research each university properly. Find out what each department specialises in. If you have a great interest in medieval history, there is no point in applying to universities that do not appear to offer this as a major element of their course.

Equally, we don't want you to be interested only in history; indication of commitment to cultural, sporting, political or charitable interests is a sign that you are a rounded individual, capable of managing your time and contributing to the community.

WHAT DOES A GOOD PERSONAL STATEMENT LOOK LIKE?

Example of a good personal statement

I have always been fascinated by history, and am enormously looking forward to the chance to devote myself to the study of different historical periods and problems at university. As part of my A2 studies this year, I have been studying England under the Tudors, a course that I have really enjoyed. I have increased my knowledge and understanding of this course in my own time by attending evening lectures by prominent historians like David Starkey. I have also taken the opportunity to read some recent books providing a broader context to my studies, and have particularly enjoyed 'Reformation: Europe's House Divided' by Diarmaid MacCulloch. My other area of particular historical interest is the Crusades and I have recently been reading 'God's War: A New History of the Crusades' by Christopher Tyerman, which offers a provocative new interpretation of the Crusades. I have also pursued my interest in medieval history by visiting castles on a recent family holiday in Wales, though I am not sure that my younger sister shared my appreciation for the finer points of fortifications!

The other subjects I am studying for A2 reinforce my interest in history. Sociology helps to provide models for human behaviour, and historians have successfully applied the theories of sociologists like Max Weber to their studies of modern societies. Studying Shakespeare's 'Richard II' for my A2 coursework in English has helped me understand the ideals of kingship that were current during the reign of Elizabeth I.

Outside my school work, I enjoy acting, and recently took the lead role in a school production of 'West Side Story'. I have also been involved in my local branch of Amnesty International, co-ordinating letter-writing campaigns for political prisoners. Fitting in these activities alongside my crowded school schedule has been hard work, but has encouraged me to manage my time effectively. I believe that this balance of work and other activities demonstrates that I will be able to flourish at university.

TOP TIPS

1 State clearly why you want to study history at university

2 Give evidence of a real enthusiasm for the subject which goes well beyond the confines of the curriculum

3 Draw appropriate connections between your chosen subject of history and your other subjects

4 Show that you have extra-curricular interests, to indicate you are a well-rounded individual who is able to balance various commitments and manage your time effectively

THINGS TO AVOID

1 Spelling and punctuation errors

2 Lazy sentence construction and a lack of coherent structure and form

3 Lies about what you claim to have read and done

4 Plagiarism

5 Poor research in the first place, leading to poor decisions – this is often apparent in a statement that lacks evidence that you understand the course and its demands

RECOMMENDED READING AND WEBSITES

- E.H. Carr, *What Is History?*, Palgrave Macmillan, 2002
- John Arnold, *A Very Short Introduction to History*, Oxford University Press, 2000
- Jeremy Black, *Studying History*, Palgrave Macmillan, 2007
- *BBC History Magazine*: www.historyextra.com
- *History Today*: www.historytoday.com
- Museums Association: www.museumsassociation.org

I am grateful for the support given to me by the History Department at Royal Holloway, University of London (www.royalholloway.ac.uk/history) in the production of this profile. Other highly rated courses include those at the universities of Oxford, Cambridge, King's College London, York and Durham.

HISTORY OF ART

This academic profile was written by an admissions tutor at The Courtauld Institute of Art, University of London. The information in this profile is useful to all applicants, but some of the advice is pertinent to that institution in particular.

SUBJECT OVERVIEW

The world is full of images, now more than ever in history. Art history mines visual and spatial artefacts – art and architecture – to gain insight into the lives of peoples, places and times both in the past and the present. As a multi-faceted historical discipline, art history is concerned with all aspects of representation and communication through visual artefacts and it relates to a number of other disciplines, from literature to film to anthropology. Art historians seek to understand how images affect us today and how they were interpreted in the past. We ask why paintings, sculpture, architecture, prints, photographs, digital media and other visual materials look the way they do and how they reflect and represent politics, religion and social concerns of the past. We deploy a range of methods and approaches to explore the circumstances under which images and visual artefacts were made, the media and techniques used, whom they were made for and what functions they performed. Given how much of our understanding of and interest in the past is formed by the historical and contemporary responses to visual artefacts, art history offers one of the key disciplines in seeking to understand the history of humankind.

Offers vary depending on the university and most departments offer the course as a single honours or part of a joint honours degree. Common combinations include history of art and history, philosophy, English, modern languages or Classics.

It is a myth that you need to have studied history of art at A level or Pre-U. Most state schools do not offer the subject, so an application without history of art will not be judged negatively.

> **❝** The course as a whole is incredibly interesting, very flexible in catering to your interests (with the ability to take modules outside of the department), and challenging. My pathway incorporated philosophical and historical approaches, in addition to chemistry and language modules! **❞**
>
> **3RD-YEAR STUDENT, UNIVERSITY COLLEGE LONDON**

WHAT SKILLS OR ATTRIBUTES DO ADMISSIONS TUTORS LOOK FOR IN A GOOD APPLICANT?

There is no expectation that you would have studied history of art for A level or Pre U, although if you have we would want to know what aspects of the course most interested you and would hope that you discuss the skills that you have acquired as part of the process. If you have not studied the subject before, just be willing to show us that you have the drive it takes to 'get out there' and look at art, design and architecture. We want you to provide evidence that your interest is real; this should be backed up by visits to galleries, and references to architectural buildings that interest you and how those link with history. Most, but not all, applicants will have studied history, and we would like you to provide evidence that you can read, write and think. We want people who are open minded and want new experiences. A good personal statement will also show us what you have done outside of the classroom. What initiatives have you taken? What opportunities have you grabbed outside school?

Finally, as the subject is essay-based, we would like you to have the analytical and evaluative skills that are best prepared for by exposure to an essay-based subject (history or English for instance) and/or a subject that has made you think and question (philosophy or psychology). We also welcome those with science backgrounds too, but want to see that you have the essay skills we need too. To that end, you may wish to reference coursework undertaken.

WHAT DOES A GOOD PERSONAL STATEMENT LOOK LIKE?

If you are committed to art history, and are aiming for a particular programme, your personal statement should be written with that institution's undergraduate admissions process and selection criteria in mind.

Everyone is surrounded by visual materials, from buildings and works of art to films, photography, fashion, advertisements and computer games. Ideally, your personal statement will include an explanation of why some visual materials you have seen really interest you. Admissions tutors look for an expression and explanation of enthusiasm for the topic of art history and for the study of visual materials as evidence of historical circumstances and human activity. You might include an account of how your understanding of visual materials has been affected by an article or book you have read (not necessarily art history). A description of how you became interested in art history and what you are looking forward to in studying the subject at university can assist the admissions tutors to better gauge your readiness for and commitment to the subject. You might also provide an analysis of how the skills and knowledge you have gained from the other subjects you have studied have prepared you for a degree in art history.

Above all, most admission tutors want to gain a clear picture of you as an individual who has the motivation and potential to benefit from a degree course in art history.

Example of a good personal statement

The candidate who wrote this statement was a mature student – a significant number of applicants to this subject are mature, in that they are often in their early 20s.

History of art is the door to artistic, cultural, historical and personal enrichment. With motivation and effort it can also lead to truly interesting career opportunities, most notably, as far as I am concerned, fine art auctioneer. It is one of the most appealing and diverse subjects you can work with, as it expresses itself through various supports. It allows you to gain access to cultures throughout the world, their beliefs and history, through a single still image, a sculpture or even a white canvas.

Art is an uncompromised, satirical and beautiful gateway to the world and the history of mankind. Art is not only beautiful, choking, impressive or aesthetic, art is a testimony of historical patrimony, and this is one of the main reasons I want to study history of art.

My interest in the subject started in my school years during which I obtained outstanding grades in history, art and literature. My passion for the subject flowed out into my social life, as I attended weekly cultural seminars organised by 'Les Amis des Arts et de la Culture' in Monaco. For personal reasons I decided not go to university after completing my Baccalaureate but this did not affect my interest in art. In my spare time I developed a great enthusiasm for photography. My grandfather taught me how to develop pictures when I was 13 and I was at once attracted to the mixture of art and information as captured by the legendary Cartier Bresson. Furthermore, being able to step away from the world and become more than a spectator was a welcome relief from a hard day's work.

TOP TIPS

1 Be honest about yourself – we want to know you, not the person you want to become

2 Be clear about why you want to study the subject and provide some evidence to support that opinion. What artists do you find yourself drawn to? Why? What galleries have you spent time in? What genre of art is your favourite?

3 Be clear about the skills you have picked up at school or college. History of art is an essay-based subject so we will look for applicants who can show an ability to write well, think clearly and be bold in the outlook

4 Everyone is surrounded by visual materials, from buildings and works of art to films, photography, fashion, advertisements and computer games. Ideally, your personal statement will include an explanation of why some visual materials you have seen really interest you

5 Do you have any career aspirations that may be helped by your study of the subject?

 THINGS TO AVOID

1 Sloppy spelling, punctuation and grammar

2 Claims that cannot be substantiated with evidence or that do not support the application

3 Lack of evidence that you are passionate about art and the creative world

4 Clichés and obvious untruths!

5 Plagiarism

 RECOMMENDED READING AND WEBSITES

- Marcia Pointon, *History of Art: A Student's Handbook*, 5th edition, Routledge, 2014
- The Art History Archive: www.arthistoryarchive.com
- Museums Association: www.museumsassociation.org

I am grateful for the support of the University of London in preparing this profile. A number of London Colleges offer history of art, the most famous being The Courtauld Institute. Other excellent courses are offered at the universities of St Andrews, Cambridge, Exeter and York.

JOURNALISM

This academic profile is a composite of information provided by admissions tutors at City University London. The information is useful to all applicants, but some of the advice is pertinent to City in particular.

SUBJECT OVERVIEW

There are several hundred journalism courses around the country, and they vary enormously. Some courses, such as the BA in Journalism at City University London, have a practical approach, equipping would-be journalists with the core skills they need, including recognising what is newsworthy, researching a story, writing and presentation – whether for the internet, print or broadcast, or all three. Other courses are more theoretical, and are more like media studies courses, with a strong element of communication theory.

Take great care to study course outlines at the various universities you are looking at to make sure you apply for the kind of course you want. If you are determined to become a journalist, then a more practical course will more likely lead to a job. Such a degree, whether as a single or joint honours with another subject such as economics, politics or history, will help towards a job in journalism as well as in related areas such as public relations and event management.

The BA Journalism course is aimed at the many students who have decided to make a career in journalism. It provides practical education and proficiency in print, broadcast and online journalism as well as relevant studies in humanities such as politics and the history of journalism.

City's Journalism BA (Hons) course has a real-world emphasis. You will learn skills such as reporting a speech, presenting a radio news broadcast, interviewing and producing news and feature stories. You will spend time developing online skills, using the TV studio and making video packages. At the same time you will pursue academic studies relevant to journalism and you will be taught by a wide range of lecturers who are experts within their field.

WHAT SKILLS OR ATTRIBUTES DO ADMISSIONS TUTORS LOOK FOR IN A GOOD APPLICANT?

A good journalist needs to be inquisitive, interested in people and in what is going on, to look into why something has happened and what its implications are. A journalist needs to have ideas, to be able to think creatively, and s/he also needs to be a good listener.

If the university holds interviews, the admissions tutors will certainly ask what papers and magazines you read and what news and current affairs programmes and websites you follow. They might want to know who your favourite journalist is – whose job you would like to have in 10 years' time.

To get onto a journalism course, students need to show that they are creative. This will often be demonstrated by written material and may also include an interest in design and photography. Admissions tutors may expect a potential student to have done some blogging, perhaps about local sport, or music, but any writing would be of interest, from poetry to a first novel.

Attention to detail is very important: although many people believe there are too many errors in newspapers, it is amazing how few there are, considering how much material is edited and put together in such a short time. A good journalist not only needs to know where to put an apostrophe, but needs to care that it is in the right place.

WHAT DOES A GOOD PERSONAL STATEMENT LOOK LIKE?

Your personal statement is the only way to show the admissions tutor that you can write well, so spend as much time as possible on it. Make the statement (and yourself) as interesting as possible. Work out what makes you different from the next applicant, and focus on that so that you stand out from the crowd. If you are determined, for example, to be a political journalist, write a bit about what interests you about politics, show that you know what is going on, mention what papers you read, talk about where you would like to work. If it is music that interests you, don't just say you like music – every young person does; talk about the particular genres that interest you, and the particular magazines or websites that you want to write for.

If you are applying to several different types of courses – perhaps politics at one university, and journalism at another – take care not to be too specific, or you will put off at least one of the admissions tutors.

Example of a good personal statement

The following personal statement demonstrates the student's talent for writing. It is well laid out, error free and punchy. Their work and extra-curricular pursuits show their enthusiasm for journalism – something which is essential throughout your career. This personal statement was written by a mature student, so some of the references may seem to be a bit dated. But that does not detract in any way from the quality of the statement.

> In 2005 I found my first love: music. The influx of new bands and my first live experiences convinced me that I had to work in the industry. As we began to do more creative writing in English, I realised that I wanted to combine these two interests. This gave me an ambition: music journalism. Later, inspired by my work in Media Studies, I set up an online music fanzine to get my reviews out there.

✓ This is a strong introduction which gives admissions tutors essential information about the student's achievements and ambitions straight away.

> June 2008 was a turning point. I was selected to attend The Tony Wilson Experience – a major event, inspiring and offering opportunity to young people through discussion with those experienced in the creative industries. There, I met a writer who offered me the chance to write for an award-winning music fanzine, 'High Voltage'. I now regularly contribute reviews and features to the online and print editions.
>
> The 'Manchester Evening News' (MEN) City Life (entertainment supplement) editor ran a contest to report on the event. Despite stiff competition, mine was chosen as winner. My work was published and I was able to organise work experience.
>
> During my time at the MEN I had four articles published. It was made even more interesting with the challenge of writing on new subjects, including art exhibitions. I did my first interview, and though nervous at first, thoroughly enjoyed the experience. Since then, contacting people to get unique quotes for articles has been instinctive.
>
> My online experience encouraged my editor to involve me in City Life's website launch. Learning about the transition was fascinating and gave me an insight into how the industry is evolving. I now regularly contribute reviews and features to Citylife.co.uk.

✓ This section is important, as it goes into more detail about the student's experience, awards and the recognition that they have received as a result of their own hard work outside of college. The student's passion for journalism, especially within the creative industries, comes through clearly, which is something that we look out for in all our students.

> At college I took music technology to gain an understanding of what makes good-quality music. Learning about how genres and recording techniques have developed made me think more analytically about music. A desire to gain a wider general knowledge made me take history and critical thinking, but I have learnt a lot about politics and persuasion. I am now better at evidencing my opinions and fascinated by religious practice in early modern Europe, visiting sites around the country to learn more.
>
> English and media studies have given me opportunities to be creative on a range of platforms. I have learnt to write in different styles and found out a lot about communication and media industries. Following my GCSE, I received my school's media award for creating an alternative gossip magazine.

✓ You will spend a lot of time doing your A levels, so it is good to demonstrate what you have learnt during your studies, even if your A levels are not related to journalism. This student highlights how they have achieved a more in-depth understanding of music through their A level in music technology – this supports their ambition of becoming a music journalist as set out at the beginning of the statement.

In my free time I swim and ski to keep fit. The college debating society helps me to explain ideas clearly. Discussing political issues (another major passion) with people of different opinions gives me new ways of looking at things.

I have been playing the guitar for eight years. My tutor, a recording artist, teaches me a lot about the music industry and theory.

On a trip to Cuba I was captivated by the culture, history and people of Havana. It renewed my childhood interest in the language, so over the summer I took an evening course to gain a basic level of Spanish.

Following volunteer work at the Plaza Theatre, I joined the Youth Action Team. Together, we promote volunteering to young people and develop new opportunities for them.

✓ Talking about your extra-curricular activities demonstrates that you are a rounded person who can manage their time. University life is busy, so the ability to balance your studies, socialising, volunteering or work experience is a key skill to have.

 TOP TIPS

1 Remember, you are applying to a course that is all about the written word. Your statement should be concise, clear and written in a vibrant style

2 Give examples of writing you have done thus far. If you have edited a school magazine, we want to know

3 Talk about your skills and how you have acquired them

4 Talk about your extra-curricular pursuits, particularly those where you need initiative and drive to succeed. Hard work is commendable!

 THINGS TO AVOID

1 Poor spelling, grammar and punctuation. Get the statement proofread by someone competent to spot these errors

2 Plagiarism – the worst sin, as this is a profession that relies on creative writing, not copying others' ideas and passing them off as your own

3 Saying anything that you could not justify or explain at interview. Many courses do interview now, as competition for places is high

4 Undersell your achievements – we want confident go-getters, not those who hide their lights under bushels

RECOMMENDED READING AND WEBSITES

- Anna McKane, *Journalism: A Career Handbook*, Methuen Drama, 2004
- Broadcast Journalism Training Council: www.bjtc.org.uk
- National Council for the Training of Journalists: www.nctj.com

I am grateful to City University London for providing the information used to prepare this profile. Other highly rated courses include those at the universities of Cardiff, University of the Arts London, Anglia Ruskin and Bournemouth.

LAW

This academic profile was written by an admissions tutor at the University of Brighton. The information in this profile is useful to all applicants, but some of the advice is pertinent to Brighton in particular.

 SUBJECT OVERVIEW

Studying law is a life-enhancing experience. Degree programmes in law provide both university experience and the opportunity to make a difference in society. Skills-based learning and extra-curricular activities empower individuals through confidence building, presentation, negotiation and advocacy skills as well as excellent networking, shadowing and work-experience opportunities. This balance of academic and work-based learning is excellent preparation for a career in the law, commerce, public service or the not-for-profit sector.

Brighton Business School offers two LLB pathways: with business or with criminology. Both are qualifying law degrees (QLDs), preparing graduates for potential careers as solicitors, barristers, paralegals, corporate lawyers, public servants and other professional legal roles. LLB students are encouraged to undertake a paid work placement in the third year, in order to gain employment experience and develop core competencies in communication, team-working, problem solving and leadership. In our experience, we find completion of the assessed placement project in Year 3 can help improve final-year performance.

WHAT SKILLS OR ATTRIBUTES DO ADMISSIONS TUTORS LOOK FOR IN A GOOD APPLICANT?

We are looking for enthusiastic people who have a good academic profile and who are prepared to learn. Our students have a wide range of educational experiences. We like to recruit students who are motivated and have made the effort to find out about how law contributes to society. We are particularly keen on people who have had the opportunity to observe different aspects of the law and are able to explain why they are interested in developing a career in the law.

Entry standards vary, but most departments now make offers of BBB (or their equivalent). At Brighton the course consists of the foundations of legal knowledge (FLKs): contract law, criminal law, equity and trusts, European law, land law, public law and tort, together with legal skills knowledge and academic skills building. In addition, students may select optional modules to tailor the course to their own ambitions and interests, including company law, intellectual property, family law, human rights and business, employment law, contemporary studies in crime and justice and cross cultural criminology. The teaching methods involve seminars, workshops and lectures, blended learning, tutorials and problem-based learning – according to what most suits the learning material.

WHAT DOES A GOOD PERSONAL STATEMENT LOOK LIKE?

It is really helpful if you have observed some interactions with the practice of law, the justice system, or the contribution of law to society; briefly describe your experience and explain why you would like to study law. You really need to describe something more varied than a personal interest in crime drama and which shows that you have made an effort to see different aspects of the law or criminal justice, or at least have plans to broaden your understanding.

It is always good to hear about your activities beyond the academic. We are interested in sport, music, drama and other extra-curricular pursuits, especially if they show evidence of individual leadership or team-work skills. If you have had a job or done voluntary work, make sure you explain something positive about the experience of interacting with people. Consider your communication skills, your ability to problem-solve and to think creatively.

Try to find a balance between self-promotion and personal commitment, explaining your recent experiences of work, social activities and school achievements. Over-emphasis on any of these elements can skew your statement.

Examples from good personal statements

> I have shadowed a local solicitor and sat in on several sessions in the magistrates' courts, where I saw a range of cases being heard. The law intrigues me as it is constantly adapting over time to coincide with our ever-changing society. I believe my study of sociology, psychology, English language, philosophy and ethics complement each other and have taught me to be more logical, and more open minded to other people's circumstances.

✓ The above statement shows that an effort has been made beyond personal experience, and that active research has been undertaken to broaden an understanding of the law and criminology in society.

> I have formed the ability to provide a unique, analytical approach to problem solving. The study of A level Law has developed the skills required to systematically construct and evaluate an argument. The study of philosophy and religion has provided transferable skills when reasoning with complex ideologies. I am interested in the philosophy of law and in exploring the ethics and moral codes in which society is bound.

✓ This statement shows a considered approach to developing a well-informed opinion.

> Outside of academic studies I have held a variety of part-time occupational roles. The most rewarding of these I consider to be as an instructor in an animal park where I acquired a sense of responsibility, developed enhanced communication skills, punctuality, reliability and organisational expertise. I thrive in a team environment but have also adapted to become an independent thinker and project worker. These skills have been furthered in my role as a form rep on the student council, where I've organised school fundraising events and submitted my own and my peers' suggestions to improve aspects of the school to the senior staff. Through these roles, I have learnt the rewards of making a positive contribution to my community and to society. I enjoy working and welcome any placement opportunities aligned to the legal profession or the criminal justice sector, as I feel this would complement and strengthen my academic studies.

✓ This shows an understanding of the key competencies employers seek and a commitment to building on these in pursuit of a placement year. Future employers are keen to identify wider experience and the defined abilities that complement a good degree.

 TOP TIPS

1 We do not expect you to know any UK law. However, we do expect you to express clearly why you want to study it and the reasons behind your decision to apply

2 We want you to show us your motivation: how you apply yourself to different tasks and how you cope with hard work and times of intense pressure

 THINGS TO AVOID

1 Plagiarism – never copy material and pass it off as you own

2 Poor sentence construction, spelling or grammar

3 No evidence of the top tips; you have to promote yourself. We assume you are clever enough – so use the statement to promote your non academic skills too

3 Try and show evidence of your reasoning ability. Can you analyse and solve problems using logical and critical approaches? Can you see the wood from the trees and the relevant from the irrelevant?

4 Provide examples of where you have shown accuracy in your work

5 Are you creative and can you adapt to different situations

6 What are you reading that is relevant to the course?

7 If you are you a good listener and are known for being a person who is able to express themselves with clarity and consideration, let us know through examples

4 Underperformance in the LNAT tests (where appropriate)

5 Clichés about the law gathered from film and TV

6 Saying that you are in it for the money – it may be true, but avoid declaring it in the personal statement!

 # RECOMMENDED READING, MEDIA AND WEBSITES

Read, watch and listen to any current affairs information about law and society.

- Melanie Allen and Steven Boyes, *Getting into Law*, Trotman Education, 2016
- *Law in Action*: www.bbc.co.uk/programmes/b006tgy1 and *Thinking Allowed*: www.bbc.co.uk/programmes/b006qy05; both on Radio 4
- Law Careers.net: www.lawcareers.net
- The Bar Standards Board: www.barstandardsboard.org.uk
- The Chartered Institute of Legal Executives: www.cilex.org.uk
- The Crown Prosecution Service: www.cps.gov.uk
- The Magistrates' Association: www.magistrates-association.org.uk

I am grateful to the University of Brighton (www.brighton.ac.uk) for its support in preparing this profile. Other highly rated courses include those at the universities of Cambridge, King's College London, Durham, York and Manchester.

MATHEMATICS

This academic profile was written by an admissions tutor at Royal Holloway, University of London. The information in this profile is useful to all applicants, but some of the advice is pertinent to that department in particular.

SUBJECT OVERVIEW

For some, mathematics is a pure science to be studied for its intrinsic beauty and logical structure. For many it means problem solving and the satisfaction of getting what is indisputably the 'right' answer. Others will consider the myriad and diverse applications of mathematics in areas such as finance or quantum information. The truth is that mathematics encompasses all these and more, because each perspective is fundamentally linked to the others.

By studying mathematics you gain a diverse range of transferable skills, including how to apply a universal language in a multiplicity of situations and see connections between them. Mathematics also provides an excellent foundation for a variety of fulfilling career paths or opportunities for further study.

WHAT SKILLS OR ATTRIBUTES DO ADMISSIONS TUTORS LOOK FOR IN A GOOD APPLICANT?

The three things that interest us most are:

- mathematics
- mathematics
- mathematics!

That is perhaps an over simplification, but your mathematical talent is by far the most important factor for admissions tutors. Of course they are also looking for an enthusiasm that will sustain you over three or four years. University study is more independent than at school, so time-management skills, determination to succeed and a good work ethic are also highly relevant. Evidence of social activities undertaken in your spare time is also useful.

WHAT DOES A GOOD PERSONAL STATEMENT LOOK LIKE?

A good personal statement is, above all, personal. It gives you the chance to speak directly to the admissions tutor about yourself, your reasons for choosing a particular degree programme, your choice of A level subjects, your personal interests and out-of-school activities; in summary, what makes you tick.

Be honest: if you say that a particular branch of mathematics interests you, or you have read a particular book, then this is likely to be a topic of discussion at interview. Talk about your current skills and attributes, particularly if they are either mathematical (you might like puzzles, chess, strategy games) or non-academic (such as leadership, initiative or examples of personal challenges that you have overcome). Include anything that you would like the admissions tutor to know about you that would not be covered elsewhere on the application form.

TOP TIPS

1 Your statement should be clear, concise and free from errors

2 Your statement should explain clearly in the opening paragraph why maths is your choice of degree and, more importantly, what evidence you can provide that supports this view

3 Mention if you have obtained high scores in tests or taken part in national maths challenges

4 Mention your non-academic attributes too – leadership, personal success in tasks and any work-experience or taster courses

5 If you have a career in mind that lends itself to maths, let us know

THINGS TO AVOID

1 Spelling and other mistakes

2 Poorly constructed sentences that do not follow logically

3 Under-emphasising your skills and why they will be suitable for maths

4 Not mentioning your work ethic and attitude to individual learning

5 Appearing to be unsociable and unwilling to engage in extra-curricular pursuits

RECOMMENDED READING AND WEBSITES

- Lara Alcock, *How to Study for a Mathematics Degree*, Oxford University Press, 2012
- Tom Körner, *The Pleasures of Counting*, Cambridge University Press, 1996. This uses examples as diverse as the outbreak of cholera in Victorian Soho, the Battle of the Atlantic, African Eve and the design of anchors to show the kinds of problems that interest mathematicians and the various ways they attack them
- Institute of Mathematics and its Applications: www.ima.org.uk
- Mathematical Association: www.m-a.org.uk

I am grateful for the support I received from the Mathematics Department at Royal Holloway, University of London (www.royalholloway.ac.uk/mathematics) in the preparation of this profile. Other highly rated courses include those at the universities of Cambridge, Oxford, Warwick, Greenwich and Leicester.

MEDICINE

This academic profile was written by an admissions tutor at Brighton and Sussex Medical School (BSMS). The information is useful to all applicants, but some of the advice is pertinent to BSMS in particular.

UCAS permits you to apply to a maximum of four medical schools. Given the competition for places, it is imperative that you use all of your application slots. I recommend that you also apply for an alternative course in your fifth slot, with biomedical science, biochemistry and neuroscience being ideal alternatives. This way you may, should you gain a good degree, be able to enter medical school via one of the popular graduate entry schemes. Applicants without the required academic profile may find it possible to gain entry to one of the Foundation courses, where a student is admitted to medical school after completing a Foundation year.

SUBJECT OVERVIEW

Becoming a doctor isn't an easy option – it takes years of study and hard work. As you learn the skills you need, you will also learn a great deal about yourself. If you like helping people there are few more rewarding or respected careers. You'll be part of a team of professionals and non-medical staff delivering care to the highest standards in the NHS. Medicine is about helping people – treating illness, providing advice and reassurance, and seeing the effects of both ill health and good health from the patient's point of view. You have to examine the symptoms presented by a patient, and consider a range of possible diagnoses of their cause. You must test your diagnosis, decide on the best course of treatment and monitor progress. This demands an enquiring mind, the capacity to acquire and maintain high levels of knowledge that have to be constantly up to date and the ability to relate to people as individuals, each with their own health needs.

If you have the passion to improve people's lives and the determination to reach the highest standards, you will have many career opportunities. You can follow a path to one of many specialties, from working in a hospital as a surgeon to being based in the community as a GP. The training and support available to you in the NHS can help you get to the very top of your chosen career.

Medicine is a demanding profession, but one that repays the hard work and dedication it involves through the rich variety of career opportunities it offers. Whether helping patients, managing a hospital or pushing back the borders of medical research, you will have the satisfaction of knowing that you are making a positive contribution to society.

At university, you will be kept busy with a mixture of seminars, lectures, anatomy classes, clinical skills practice and patient interaction, depending on where you study. In later years you will spend more time with medical teams than in the classroom. Assessments may be through exams, written portfolios or practical tests. Medical students are also known for their busy social lives!

WHAT SKILLS OR ATTRIBUTES DO ADMISSIONS TUTORS LOOK FOR IN A GOOD APPLICANT?

You will need the ability, the commitment and the personal qualities necessary to become an excellent doctor. Academically, BSMS requires three A levels at grade A, to include biology and chemistry. In addition to three A levels our standard offer will include an additional AS at grade B or the Extended Project Qualification (EPQ), again at grade B. If applicants attend a school or college that does not provide the opportunity for either of these options they should contact BSMS. Many equivalent qualifications are accepted, depending on whether you have studied abroad, or already completed a degree. Most medical schools also require you to take the Biomedical Admissions Test (BMAT: www.bmat.org.uk) or UK Clinical Aptitude Test (UKCAT: www.ukcat.co.uk).

Just as important are a realistic attitude to medical training and clinical practice, a commitment to caring for others, the ability to communicate and work effectively within a team and to appreciate other people's point of view, and a willingness to accept responsibility.

WHAT DOES A GOOD PERSONAL STATEMENT LOOK LIKE?

Medicine is a diverse profession with specialties that suit a wide range of people. We want our student body to reflect the variety of the profession and of society as a whole, and are not looking for any one model of personal statement.

Your personal statement should contain a short introduction about why you want to study medicine. Indicate what relevant experience you have, perhaps with a GP, in a hospital, hospice, care home or with disabled groups, and how you have reflected on and learnt from it. This work experience is hard to achieve but the fact that you have it will tell us that you have the drive and passion to succeed.

Do let us know what you learnt from the work experience rather than just telling us what you did. The tutor will be looking for evidence that you know what it is like to be a doctor and know a bit about healthcare delivery. We need to weed out those who think it is like *ER* or *Holby City*!

Demonstrate your understanding of scientific and medical issues; regular reading will help. We suggest that you read quite widely, particularly in the lead-up to your interview. You ought to be aware of issues in medicine that you will have heard discussed in broadsheet newspapers and scientific journals.

Include not only what you have learnt through study but your other activities and non-academic achievements – sports, hobbies, travel, awards and so on. Show what relevant qualities you have developed from your experiences, for example in communicating, leadership or team-work.

Avoid poor spelling, grammar and punctuation. This leaves a poor impression and, while it is not hugely significant, you cannot really afford to be seen as careless when competition is so fierce.

 TOP TIPS

1 Find out as much as you can about what it is like to be a doctor. Talk to healthcare professionals, read as much as you can and try to get some relevant work experience. Mention what you have learnt as a result in the statement and be willing to discuss it at interview

 THINGS TO AVOID

1 Making any claims in your personal statement that you cannot substantiate at interview

2 Plagiarising any part of your personal statement – when admissions tutors read through over 1,000 applications this soon becomes obvious

2 Research the prospectuses and websites of a variety of medical schools, and visit some to make sure you find the course, teaching styles, facilities and location that are right for you

3 Begin work on your personal statement early – the UCAS deadline for medicine courses is earlier than for other university programmes. Get comments from other people and write several drafts. Make sure you are happy with it before you submit it to UCAS

4 Read the BMA's excellent guide to Becoming a Doctor, which you can download at the BMA website www.bma.org.uk

3 Taking an inflexible stance on contentious issues – you need to be able to work with people who hold all kinds of opinions

4 Memorising set answers to the interview questions you think you might get – the interviewers will be able to get to know you better through a natural conversation

5 Going into medicine because other people want you to – don't succumb to their pressure if you don't feel it's the right choice for you

---

RECOMMENDED READING AND WEBSITES

- James Barton and Simon Horner, *Getting into Medical School*, Trotman Education, 2016
- Becoming a Doctor, BMA website: www.bma.org.uk
- General Medical Council: www.gmc-uk.org
- Med Schools Online: www.medschoolsonline.co.uk – this excellent website has up-to-date advice about preparing a great application
- Want to be a Doctor: www.wanttobeadoctor.co.uk – a fantastic website that provides great advice about applications to this competitive course
- Faculty of Public Health: www.fph.org.uk
- Royal College of General Practitioners: www.rcgp.org.uk
- Royal College of Surgeons of England: www.rcseng.ac.uk
- Skills for Health: www.skillsforhealth.org.uk

I am grateful to the Brighton and Sussex Medical School (www.bsms.ac.uk) for its help in preparing this profile. There are a number of other universities that offer medicine and they are all regulated by the GMC. A full list can be found on the UCAS website (www.ucas.com).

MIDWIFERY

This academic profile was written by an admissions tutor at Swansea University and draws upon information from other course prospectuses too. The information in this profile is useful to all applicants, but some of the advice is pertinent to Swansea in particular.

SUBJECT OVERVIEW

Midwives offer individual care to women and their families and help them take part in their own care planning during pregnancy. Both during and after pregnancy you will be with the new mother in her own locality.

Midwifery is as much about supporting the new mother and her partner as it is about helping with the birth of the baby. Support continues from the confirmation of the pregnancy through to the postnatal days after the baby is born.

Student midwives work towards providing a service that is effective and satisfying for women and their families. Many women are cared for exclusively by midwives throughout their pregnancy, childbirth and the postnatal period. Midwifery is therefore a very responsible career, but it has incredible rewards to offset the dedication required.

The philosophy of a degree course in midwifery is to prepare a midwife who is able to practise from the point of registration. It is designed to build upon an individual's strengths and to value her life experiences to develop into a professional and motivated practitioner. Students develop a heightened level of self-awareness and sensitivity towards women and their families throughout the programme.

The learner is expected to grow in confidence and self-awareness; to take responsibility for their personal and professional development. Students then emerge into the practice arena as lifelong learners – confident, competent and accountable for their own practice as a midwife meeting the challenges of contemporary practice.

The new graduate will get to see the miracle of new life on a daily basis. From measuring pregnancy bumps to taking command during labour, hearing the first squawk of a new arrival and then visiting them during their first few weeks – most midwives say they couldn't have a more satisfying job! However, the hours are tough and the pay isn't fantastic, especially when you consider how important experts in this field are. At degree level, students of midwifery get front-line and academic experience of how to lead women and babies through such a crucial stage of life.

WHAT SKILLS OR ATTRIBUTES DO ADMISSIONS TUTORS LOOK FOR IN A GOOD APPLICANT?

Candidates need to be caring and understanding individuals with a sensitive nature. Good communication skills are essential in this career. Most midwives are committed, extremely motivated and usually female. Being non-squeamish, staunchly practical and having a 'no nonsense' attitude is a must.

Most candidates in the UK who wish to enter the degree programme at Swansea must have achieved three A levels at grade B or above, maths and a science at GCSE grade B or above. This is common to most departments, but all good departments welcome applicants who have life experience and we tend to attract a fair number of mature students. As such, we do vary our offers from time to time to meet the needs of different applicants.

All students must be able to demonstrate key skills and numeracy. These requirements will vary between institutions. At the top end, King's College London asks for ABB at A level. You'll need a clean Disclosure and Barring Service record and occupational health clearance to get into any course in the UK.

Many departments, including Swansea, due to the competition for a small number of places, cannot consider applications for deferred entry. You should also expect to be interviewed by most departments. They will expect a candidate to have a good working knowledge of the profession and of issues relating to it.

WHAT DOES A GOOD PERSONAL STATEMENT LOOK LIKE?

You should write convincingly about your clear understanding of the role of the midwife and how your experience and attributes fit well with a career in midwifery. You should research the demands of the role and current NHS practice so that you can demonstrate your awareness of the role in the opening part of your personal statement, and show that you understand that midwives work with people from all walks of like and often in stressful situations. This may, but does not have to, involve some work experience or personal contact with a practising midwife.

We like to see evidence of the key skills required, both academic and non-academic, and would like to hear what particular skills you have developed in your A level or equivalent studies. The sciences are important to emphasise, but we do also look for breadth – make sure that you know the academic demands of each department you apply to before writing your statement. We also look for clarity, good spelling and grammar and evidence that you are involved in a wide range of extra-curricular pursuits.

Please do not list skills without explaining why they are relevant, present a sloppy statement that is full of errors of just say that you like watching *Call the Midwife*!

Example of a good personal statement

Midwifery became my passion at the age of 10, when my step-mother became pregnant. This sparked off my fascination with all aspects of pregnancy, insisting that I attended every antenatal appointment that I could. From this I discovered what a vital role midwives play in caring for mother and baby in the months leading up to the birth, the labour and the postnatal period.

After having this interest for quite some time, I feel my aim now is to prosper in this subject by attending a university course; this will enable me to gain a greater understanding of the medical and practical side of midwifery. As two of my core qualities are to care and nurture, I feel I possess two of the vital attributes to pursue a career within the health professions and my aspiration for a career in midwifery is reflected in my A level choices, where good time keeping, self-motivated study skills and ability to cope under pressure and stress are essential. From studying biology I have gained further knowledge of human biology, learning more about how our major body organs function and genes and genetic engineering. I found this particularly interesting as it is linked to reproduction. Since studying psychology, I have gained a better understanding of people and how their minds perform. I can apply this knowledge to the way I interact and understand people in certain situations as my interpersonal skills have been expanded. Both of these subjects tested my ability to recall large volumes of knowledge, which has given me practice for similar situations that I will face whilst studying for a degree. Studying modules in health and social care, such as communication and values, and positive care environments has given me a greater awareness of how to communicate verbally and physically to people, and how this is interpreted by them. Investigating disease has made me conscious of how easily diseases are spread, their effects and ways of preventing them. This is particularly important when working in a hospital environment, and being around pregnant women and young babies, as they are highly susceptible to infections. I am currently working on an Extended Project Qualification. My title is 'What are the risks associated with teenage pregnancy and what are the roles of their midwives?' Whilst carrying out this project I have learnt more about the challenges midwives face, and how they overcome them. It has also given me an insight into a specialist area of midwifery, caring for young people.

Outside my academic studies, I volunteer at my local hospital. My role is to hand out beverages to the patients, and talk to them. This is important as it boosts their morale. I regularly volunteer on the maternity and gynaecology ward, and have experience on many other wards. This has given me an insight into the roles of different health professionals, and allowed me to witness part of the process of midwifery. From this I have become more confident and comfortable in a hospital setting, and have a greater awareness of current NHS practices. This experience has also expanded my interpersonal and communication skills, I feel it also represents the committed and caring attitude of my personality.

I have a part-time job in a clothes shop. From working in a retail environment and coming into contact with members of the public I have learnt how to work under pressure. It has also improved my organisational and time-keeping skills and demonstrated the hard-working side of my character.

I am excited by the prospect of having a high level of responsibility and independence that corresponds with university life. I am aware of the demands and challenges that I will face during my studies and within a medical career, but my commitment and desire to become a midwife has been strengthened by my life and work experiences and the job satisfaction that I will gain from it.

 # TOP TIPS

1 Do all that you can to access information to lead you to really understand the rigours of a career in midwifery and the demands of a three-year midwifery degree

2 Be prepared to explain all of this in your statement and in the interview

3 Show us that you have the academic potential to cope with the demands of the subject, by alluding to these skills in your statement

 # THINGS TO AVOID

1 Referring too much to your own birth experiences (if you have any)

2 Applying to become a midwife if your real interest lies in caring for babies and children

3 Spelling, punctuation and grammar mistakes – make sure that your statement is read carefully by another person before you submit it. Check that the spell-check is set to UK as default

 # RECOMMENDED READING AND WEBSITES

- Wendy Reed, *Getting into Nursing & Midwifery Courses*, Trotman Education, 2013
- Penny Armstrong and Sheryl Fieldman, *A Midwife's Story*, London: Pinter & Martin, 2006
- The Nursing and Midwifery Council: www.nmc.org.uk
- Royal College of Nursing: www.rcn.org.uk

I am grateful to the Midwifery department at Swansea University (www.swansea.ac.uk/undergraduate/courses/human-and-health-sciences/bmidhonsmidwifery) for its support in preparing this profile. Other highly rated courses can be found at the universities of Sheffield Hallam, Glasgow Caledonian, Leeds, Manchester and King's College London.

MODERN LANGUAGES

This academic profile was written with the help of the universities of Surrey and Birmingham. The information is useful to all applicants, but some of the advice is pertinent to those departments in particular.

SUBJECT OVERVIEW

❝ How can we understand another society and, by comparison, learn more about our own? The key is mastery of the language. From this starting point, you can examine a country's history, its literature and culture. **❞**

DR CRAIG BLUNT, FRENCH STUDIES, BIRMINGHAM

Modern language courses in the UK tend towards the languages that are studied in most UK schools, namely French, German, Spanish and Italian. They can be studied as a single subject or as part of a joint honours degree. Popular combinations include modern languages with business, politics, economics, media studies, law, anthropology and history.

Other languages on offer in UK universities include Russian, Arabic, Hebrew, Mandarin, Persian, Welsh, Japanese, Portuguese, Basque, Galician, Greek (modern) and the Nordic languages. Some departments also offer specialist courses on translation and modules designed to help prepare you for a career as an interpreter, which is growing in popularity with the expansion of the EU and UN. They are also employed in many corporate contexts.

If you study single honours you will concentrate on one subject for all four years. In your first two years you will also often take one module chosen from a wide range across the university, but apart from that your studies will be devoted to a single subject. For combinations of two languages, you would normally apply to read a BA in Modern Languages. In joint honours programmes you will study one modern language equally weighted with another subject that is not a modern language.

Spending a year abroad is a common element of language courses. This can be extremely beneficial, as immersing yourself in a language as a resident of that country extends your knowledge significantly. This option is not cheap, so bear that in mind when you apply.

However, it is far cheaper to study in the UK with a year abroad than it is to apply to study abroad for all three or four years. This is because although tuition fees can be lower in the EU, the cost of living is not met by loans from the government. You cannot normally claim a loan for study abroad, unless it is part of a UK degree.

WHAT SKILLS OR ATTRIBUTES DO ADMISSIONS TUTORS LOOK FOR IN A GOOD APPLICANT?

Usually the entry requirements are largely self-evident, in that you need a language to A level (or equivalent), but some courses allow you to start a language from the beginning. In fact, you can do pretty much all the languages from beginner's level (sometimes called *ab initio*) – apart from French at Birmingham – but only in particular combinations. This is particularly true where the language is not something that is offered in mainstream schools in the UK.

For instance, if you're doing two modern languages you need to have one to A level, but you could start the other from beginner's level. This is a common feature of many courses in the UK. For example, you might have German to A level, but you want to pick up Italian or Portuguese from scratch. You obviously wouldn't be able to start a single honours language course such as German studies from beginner's level, though. You would need an A level in that language.

It is distinctions like these that are important to note, and it shows why researching your course is so vital. Every course and every university will have different entry routes. Do the work in advance so that you find the best fit for you!

Every year about 5% of our applicants apply for courses for which they don't have the requisite qualifications and waste a choice on their UCAS forms. In a lot of cases it's because they have not done enough research before completing their UCAS application.

Non-academic traits include a sound mind, an evident zest for life and an interest in languages and cultures. We need to see some evidence of this when we read a personal statement or interview a candidate. If you have travelled abroad recently, we would like to know (other than if it was just for a sand and sea holiday!).

We are also interested to hear from students who are bilingual and have English as a second language.

WHAT DOES A GOOD PERSONAL STATEMENT LOOK LIKE?

Over the past four to five years, school teachers have become more aware that applying to university is increasingly competitive, and they need to give more help and support to applicants with getting their personal statements right. What this seems to have done is to create quite a number of 'template' personal statements that all look very much like each other. One of the things I recommend is to go for something a little different, without being idiosyncratic. Punctuation and grammar are also vital, especially if the course is competitive.

If you say you're interested in languages, we want to know why you're interested in the course. What sparked that interest? What have you done to show that interest in a real way? For example, if you've been doing extra reading around the A level curriculum, say so. Refer to books or magazines that you have read, or read in the native language. What films in a foreign language have you watched? This is easier now with the ease of access to streamed films on the internet.

Mention foreign travel, exchanges that you have been on or any other pertinent information that supports your case. If you are already bilingual, say so. It will give us an indication that you have a talent for languages, even if the languages that you speak are not those that you hope to read. Also mention career aspirations if the course will enable you to meet them. This is positive, as it indicates that you are willing to learn for a reason, not just for the sake of it.

We're also looking for applicants who are likely to adapt to the university way of thinking. We're looking for a critical mind-set, students who will be enquiring and analytical, and willing to get involved in intellectual debate. We like those who can convey that sense of excitement at getting involved in an intellectual debate. Have you done any debating in a foreign language?

Examples from good personal statements

> My decision to study French and Spanish stems not only from a genuine desire to further my knowledge, but also because of the experiences I have already had through using foreign languages.

✓ Relates past positive reactions of language learning to future chosen course of study.

> I have chosen to study French because I am passionate about language learning. In my French studies I particularly enjoy learning about French culture. One topic I found particularly interesting was 'Immigration and Multiculturalism' and how successfully North African immigrants, for instance, are integrated into French society.

✓ Shows openness to other cultures, multicultural perspectives.

Through studying Spanish at A level I have learnt a great deal about the history of Spain, with topics such as the Spanish Civil War and the reign of Franco. I am also fascinated by Spanish culture and have learnt about the architecture of Gaudi and the art of the Flamenco.

During my German studies I went on a 5-day trip to Strasbourg, Freiburg and Baden Baden. A visit to the European Parliament – where the best interpreters and translators work – has given me a good insight into what an interpreter's career entails.

✓ Concrete evidence of unearthing vocational applications of languages.

 TOP TIPS

1 Think hard about what you want to do before you start to write your personal statement

2 Think about what you enjoy and what you love and express this in your statement

3 If you are applying for a language, we need to know that you have the aptitude to succeed. Mention in your statement your current level of fluency, the experience you have of speaking the language with native speakers and any exchange trip you may have been involved in

4 Make sure that your personal statement is clear, concise, free from basic errors and sells yourself in a compelling manner

5 Mention any career aspirations that are relevant to your choices

 THINGS TO AVOID

1 Lying on your personal statement – lies are often found out and this can lead to the reject bin or worse!

2 Plagiarising from another statement – be inspired by exemplars, but ultimately be yourself! UCAS checks personal statements for signs of plagiarism and informs the university if it is suspicious

3 Spelling, punctuation and grammar errors on your statement. This is just lazy

4 Applying before you have done the right research – check the entry requirements and make sure that the course on offer plays to your strengths

5 Glib, generalised comments – they often irritate. It is a professional document and the language should be professional in tone, not too conversational or text-speak-like!

 RECOMMENDED READING AND WEBSITES

▪ You should read a range of different publications in the language you wish to study – newspapers, magazines (both serious and glossy), books and even comic books

▪ Watch films and TV in the language that you are studying – these are easy to access online

- The European Commission offers five-month training periods for graduates and up-to-date information on the latest EU legislation and policies: www.ec.europa.eu/index_en.htm
- The British Council lists opportunities for studying and working abroad in over 100 countries in the arts, education and society: www.britishcouncil.org
- The Foreign and Commonwealth Office provides paid work experience and graduate schemes: www.gov.uk/government/organisations/foreign-commonwealth-office
- The Chartered Institute of Linguists offers accredited specialist diplomas and certificates for linguists in Translation, Interpreting, Bilingual Skills and Languages for Business: www.ciol.org.uk
- The Institute of Translation and Interpreting offers networking and career development opportunities for members in areas such as language, translation, interpreting, business and technology: www.iti.org.uk

I would like to acknowledge the support of the University of Surrey (www.surrey.ac.uk) and the University of Birmingham (www.birmingham.ac.uk) in producing this profile. Other highly rated courses can be found at the universities of Oxford, Cambridge, University College London, Bath and Southampton.

MUSIC

This academic profile was written by admissions tutors at the University of Southampton. The information is useful to all applicants, but some of the advice is pertinent to that department in particular.

At this point I would like to point out that you could also, if you think it is appropriate for you, apply to read music at one of the conservatoires. These are specialist music colleges with a strong emphasis on musical performance, conducting and composition. A very high level of musical aptitude is expected. Competition is fierce and you should apply only if you have the endorsement of your music teacher as they will be asked for a reference and you will need to audition. Grade 8 Merit or Distinction is the *minimum* entry standard. You do *not* need to have studied music at A level and entry is not usually dependent on A level grades. You will be made an unconditional offer in most cases.

Applications are made direct to the conservatoire or via the UCAS Conservatoires system. Please see Chapter 10 of this book for more information.

SUBJECT OVERVIEW

Studying music at university is like Christmas coming early all the year round. Everyone who contemplates a music degree will have been bitten by the music bug from an early age, and will have been spending most of their free time at school developing instrumental and vocal skills, learning about music and how to write it, and participating in ensembles from garage bands to symphony orchestras. At university, you get to continue this passion, except that you get to do it full time. There is no subject on offer at university with such a clear match between reality and your ambitions.

At Southampton, in line with most departments, you study with world-leading academics, composers and performers who are working at the top of their field. Flexible programmes allow you to pursue your ambitions in a wide range of academic and practical subjects, combining the advantages of a stimulating and broad-based university education with excellent practical training. You can tailor the course to suit you, with a greater or lesser emphasis on performance. A level Music is a common entry requirement but not compulsory – so do your research. Many, but not all, colleges will ask you to audition.

Music is studied alone or in combination with a variety of other subjects as a joint honours course. At Southampton it is offered as a BA in Music and in combination with French, English, philosophy, acoustics, maths, management and philosophy. You can also take music with a year abroad – a popular and therefore hard-to-achieve offer.

From your first day at university, you'll be engaged in understanding how music works and translating that understanding into the performances you want to give. You'll be taught by experts in your field and given lots of opportunities to display your knowledge in public performances in front of your peers and the rest of the community.

Career prospects for music graduates are excellent, since they are equipped with the crucial qualities of communication and self-expression, interaction and team-work, and time management. Our graduates go on to careers in teaching, media, arts administration, performance, composition, journalism, production and sound engineering, and postgraduate study.

WHAT SKILLS OR ATTRIBUTES DO ADMISSIONS TUTORS LOOK FOR IN A GOOD APPLICANT?

We look for applicants with excellent A level results and with experience and abilities outside their A level curriculum. The grade requirement will depend on the nature of the course you are applying for.

But a good applicant will also have a sustained profile in instrumental and vocal performance (any style or genre), with evidence of an ability to perform in public both as a soloist and as an ensemble player. This means you have to be an extrovert soloist but at the same time a team player able to work with your colleagues. Most applicants have A level Music (or an equivalent), but not all.

WHAT DOES A GOOD PERSONAL STATEMENT LOOK LIKE?

- Be specific about your skills and experiences.
- What instruments do you play and to what level?
- Whom have you studied with?
- What ensembles are you part of, and how long have you been a member?
- How does the practical work tie in with your A level academic work? For academic courses in particular, do mention additional reading you've done around the subject, including what you've learnt from it.
- Write reflectively about the insights, skills and knowledge you've gained from a select few experiences.
- Show team-work skills.

 TOP TIPS

1 Show us that you have made a personal investment in music beyond school and make this clear in the body of your personal statement

2 Convince us that you have a genuine interest in understanding music and not just listening to it or performing it

 THINGS TO AVOID

1 Being a specialist who only plays and listens to one type of music – you need to be receptive to many musical styles and approaches to studying music in order to succeed in a music degree

2 A statement that is poorly written in terms of style and design. It should be treated as a very important document

3 Find out about the specific content of each university's course, and think carefully about which one best matches your interest: a candidate who has taken the trouble to research what we offer and is really enthused by it will come across well. This research will be evident in your statement

4 Approach us with a real understanding of what it is like to study music at university, and show us how your experiences so far have prepared you for or encouraged you towards a music degree

5 Don't play down your other strengths and interests: we're looking for students who excel not just in music, but have performed well across their school curriculum. Ideally, give some thought to how your study of maths or English or media or whatever has enhanced your appreciation of music!

and be given the time and effort that it deserves

3 Writing what you think we want to hear, if it is not you. The real you will study at university and a false impression given in the statement will only hinder you in the long term

RECOMMENDED READING AND WEBSITES

- Arts Council England: www.artscouncil.org.uk
- Associated Board of the Royal Schools of Music: www.abrsm.org
- *Gramophone*: www.gramophone.co.uk

I am grateful to the Music Department at the University of Southampton (www.southampton.ac.uk/music/index.page) for its assistance in writing this profile. Other highly rated courses can be found at the universities of Birmingham, Bristol, Cambridge, Nottingham and King's College London.

NURSING

This academic profile was written by admissions tutors at Swansea University. The information contained within this profile is useful to all applicants, but please be aware that some of the advice is pertinent to that department in particular. For

details of all nursing courses you are directed to the UCAS course search facility, which lists all the courses on offer in UK institutions.

SUBJECT OVERVIEW

Nursing is more than just a job; it's a career with a huge range of opportunities for anyone with the passion to make a difference.

Nursing is a unique occupation and offers you a chance to help others when they need it most. There has never been a more exciting time to join the nursing profession. Nurses are crucial members of a multi-professional healthcare team. Furthermore, the number and variety of nursing roles is extensive.

Once qualified as a registered nurse, you will have opportunities to work in a range of environments including NHS and independent hospitals, GP surgeries, clinics, nursing and residential homes, occupational health services, voluntary organisations, the armed forces and industry.

Today there are greater opportunities for nurses to take increased responsibility for patient care and to become specialists and advanced practitioners in many areas, for example, intensive care, cancer care and mental health.

Nursing degrees come in different forms. The most popular is adult nursing, but you can also do courses that will help you to specialise in child or mental health nursing too. Some universities, including Swansea, offer joint honours courses within the Nursing Faculty. These include healthcare sciences, health and social care and the DipHE in Paramedic Science. This latter course is designed to train paramedics to work on ambulances.

My nursing degree is split, with 50% of my time in uni with lectures, practicals, and clinical skills building, and 50% on clinical placement. So far I have had a mixture of assignments – some 2,000-and 4,000-word reflective accounts, placements (three in all and all very different), and two exams. I would recommend the course to any individual interested in nursing and caring for others.

1ST-YEAR STUDENT, SWANSEA UNIVERSITY

WHAT SKILLS OR ATTRIBUTES DO ADMISSIONS TUTORS LOOK FOR IN A GOOD APPLICANT?

Candidates need the desire to help people. You have to be a practical individual and know how to manage your time. You will, as a nurse, develop effective communication skills and the ability to work in a team, but also act as a leader.

Candidates need to demonstrate a strong educational profile and a clear commitment to their chosen branch of nursing. GCSE profiles need to include a minimum of five passes, including English language, mathematics and a physical science or double award science at grade A–C. Some universities expect more than others. Do the research when making your shortlist.

Candidates for adult nursing at Swansea typically require BBB at A level or equivalent. Each course is different, so look at this carefully before making your choice. Most courses would expect at least one A level grade B (or above) in biology or chemistry.

A level is not the only route and Swansea actively supports applicants with alternative qualifications, including:

- BTEC National Diploma Health Studies – MMM
- BTEC Higher Diploma Health Science – Pass
- Access to Health/ Nursing/ Science – this should be passed in all core subjects and a minimum of 6 passes, 33 merits and 6 distinctions.

All applicants need to demonstrate success in their studies during the previous three to five years. Although no specific subjects are required it is beneficial to study health- or science-related courses. Also, care experience may be beneficial. Mature candidates (over 23 years of age) are encouraged to apply, and have different entry routes.

Applicants are required to demonstrate evidence of their ability to read and comprehend in English or Welsh and to communicate effectively in writing. As part of the interview process applicants are required to write a brief essay. Applicants also need to demonstrate competency in numeracy, therefore they will need to take a short numeracy test on their interview day.

All students starting their programme will need Disclosure and Barring Service clearance. This is essentially a police check to ensure that you are deemed to be an appropriate adult to work with children or vulnerable adults. There is a fee of this which the student must pay. You will also need to complete an occupational health check and to have received a range of vaccinations before the course starts. This is mandatory for all UK nursing courses.

Note: You are very likely to be interviewed, so make sure that you prepare for this and that you are able to comment on anything that you disclose in your application, including in your personal statement. Good preparation might include: visiting the department's website for information on the numeracy test, participating in a mock interview and receiving feedback, reading around broad issues relating to nursing and healthcare, ensuring familiarity with your personal statement.

WHAT DOES A GOOD PERSONAL STATEMENT LOOK LIKE?

It is helpful if the applicant can write about the skills he/she has developed and demonstrate how these skills may be transferable to nursing, for example, skills in communication, team-working, organisation, information technology and leadership.

The applicant will also be well advised to be able to justify why he/she has decided to apply for a particular branch of nursing and to highlight any particular interpersonal skills and any positions of responsibility held.

It may also be helpful for the applicant to show how subjects studied at A level may be applicable to nursing. If the applicant has care experience he/she may wish to convey what has been learnt from this experience.

It is increasingly common for applicants to show work experience in a caring context. This does not need to be in an NHS hospital, although evidence that you have spoken to nurses in a hospital context will be expected on the application. You may have worked in a care home as a volunteer, in a play group with children who are disabled or as part of hospice visiting team.

Some universities will score your personal statement against their specific selection criteria – so make sure you take a look at individual university websites, as these criteria may be listed for you to refer to.

 ## TOP TIPS

1 Show an awareness of the positive and negative sides to nursing

2 Read a good newspaper to learn about changes to NHS regulations

 ## THINGS TO AVOID

1 A poorly presented UCAS application or personal statement. There is no excuse for poor spelling or basic punctuation mistakes

3 Explain clearly how you arrived at the decision to study nursing. Why, specifically, did you apply for this course (adult, child, etc.)?

4 Ensure that there are no errors of spelling or grammar in your application and check that details are correct

5 Show that you have the character as well as the academic ability to thrive in nursing

6 Ensure that what you write in your personal statement is clearly expressed and establish early on your motivation and commitment to study and to the programme

2 Bland, generic statements such as 'I always wanted to be a nurse'

3 Showing no awareness of the current politic issues that surround the NHS – for instance the move to seven-day working. Look this up!

4 Using 'text' speak in your application, particularly your personal statement. This is a professional document and the tone should be professional too

5 Failing to mention any work experience or contact with healthcare professionals that you have completed

RECOMMENDED READING AND WEBSITES

- Wendy Reed, *Getting into Nursing & Midwifery Courses*, Trotman Education, 2013
- The Nursing and Midwifery Council: www.nmc.org.uk
- Royal College of Nursing: www.rcn.org.uk

I am grateful for the support I received from the Nursing Department at Swansea University (www.swansea.ac.uk) in the preparation of this profile. Other highly regarded courses can be found at the universities of Edinburgh, Liverpool, King's College London, East Anglia and Brighton.

OCEANOGRAPHY

This academic profile was written by an admissions tutor at the University of Southampton. The information is useful to all applicants, but some of the advice is pertinent to that department in particular. Degrees in this discipline are taught at universities with a marine location and are specialist in nature. Most are BSc or MSc single honours but some are also joined up with geography, natural science or marine biology.

SUBJECT OVERVIEW

> I walk into our control room, with its panoply of views of the sea. There are the updated global pictures from the remote sensors on satellites, there are the evolving maps of subsurface variables, there are the charts that show the position and status of all our Slocum scientific platforms, and I am satisfied that we are looking at the ocean more intensely and more deeply than anyone anywhere else.

HENRY STOMMEL, THE SLOCUM MISSION, 1989

The above statement by Henry Stommel summarises the fundamental changes that oceanography has experienced in the last two decades as a result of the major advances in marine technology. Studying oceanography involves interdisciplinary studies and research in estuarine, coastal and open-ocean environments. Oceanography includes many scientific fields such as physics, geology, chemistry, biology, meteorology, geography and geodesy. In addition to oceanography, a broad range of course opportunities are available involving different disciplines and technologies, from remote sensing to molecular biology.

Because being an oceanographer is about studying the ocean, most oceanographers spend a great deal of time at sea. During the degree, lectures provide the theoretical background to the subject area, and laboratory practicals and fieldwork provide hands-on training in experimental activities and surveying techniques. During the degree, students have the opportunity to conduct real-time studies in coastal waters of the UK and abroad using advanced underwater instrumentation. These involve the application of knowledge acquired in biological, chemical, physical and geological processes, deep-sea biology, satellite technology, ocean modelling, fish biology, ocean optics, biodiversity and marine molecular biology.

All students receive training in professional key skills such as scientific writing, oral presentations and poster presentations, which are key to excelling and succeeding as a professional oceanographer, regardless of the career path the student chooses to take. Being taught by academics who are active researchers, students acquire first-hand learning about the latest developments in oceanography. In summary, this is an exciting time to be an oceanographer!

Southampton is one of the leading providers in the UK. The strength and prestige of our degree will open doors to a wide spectrum of employers who recognise graduates of our Ocean and Earth Science programme as well-qualified scientists with excellent personal and transferable skills in numeracy, communication and team-working.

Our graduates with degrees in oceanography are acknowledged as having a greater level of independence and self-reliance than comparable graduates. A degree in the Ocean and Earth Sciences will prepare you for a wide choice of careers, such as civil engineering and construction, exploration, geophysical survey projects, conservation and government.

WHAT SKILLS OR ATTRIBUTES DO ADMISSIONS TUTORS LOOK FOR IN A GOOD APPLICANT?

Entry requirements vary, but most good courses expect an applicant to have a good science background and a demonstrable interest in marine biology or oceanography. A standard offer would be ABB (or the equivalent), to include biology and one other science A level, unless maths or geology was offered.

You should display a drive and enthusiasm for – and an informed understanding of – the degree programme(s) for which you have applied. You should be able to demonstrate that you have thoroughly researched the subject area and have considered why you wish to undertake such a degree in the context of your future career development. You will be expected to have ensured that your academic background and the examinations you have yet to take are acceptable, and that your qualifications will be of a sufficient level of attainment to ensure admission to the course of your choice.

You should provide sufficient information in your personal statement to indicate that you not only appreciate the personal skills and abilities required for successful completion of an earth science degree, but that you can illustrate such an appreciation with pertinent personal examples in the form of education-based experience (for example, personal and team-based sporting or musical activities), extra-curricular or work experience. If you can, provide evidence or demonstrate well-developed time and personal management skills, English language, grammar and numerical skills, along with a degree of independence; these are all aspects of your character that will be of interest to admissions staff.

WHAT DOES A GOOD PERSONAL STATEMENT LOOK LIKE?

Your personal statement should provide an admissions tutor with sufficient information to convey that you have not only a drive and enthusiasm for the degree programme(s) for which you are applying, but also that you have thoroughly researched the subject area and have considered why you wish to undertake such a degree in the context of your future career development. As a potential applicant you will be expected to tailor your personal statement to address your interest in the wider subject discipline, and perhaps in specific areas of the discipline. To realise this you may choose to draw upon your own experiences in A level subjects, involvement in subject-related extra-curricular activities or work experience. This part of the statement ought to comprise some 30–50% of the whole statement, and should be reflective and demonstrate self-awareness.

As all earth and marine science subject areas will have a practical, field-based component, you ought to highlight any such experience and skills which you already have, be they study based (for example, A levels), or extra-curricular (for example, Duke of Edinburgh Award scheme, Operation Raleigh or activity-style holidays you have organised for yourself).

However, many of the personal skills and abilities required for successful completion of an earth or marine science degree can also be demonstrated by reference to other forms of education-based experience (for example, personal and individual/team-based sporting or musical activities) or work experience. Avoid meaningless literary quotes or apparently deep, thoughtful insights about your chosen topic that you have picked off a website or invented – admissions tutors have read most of them already!

Example of a good personal statement

I have always been fascinated by how the different landscapes in our world have been shaped and formed by the physical workings of the planet. I am particularly interested in oceanography, physical geography and the earth systems, including plate tectonics. My study of the mechanisms of river and coastal processes has inspired me to research physical and human impact on the environment. The current debate around climate change adds a further dimension to my interests. I look forward to exploring the political and ethical elements involved in the debate with equally enthusiastic tutors and fellow students.

I have enjoyed developing my team-work skills on field trips to Lulworth Cove and at Slapton. In Slapton, I collected river data along the river Lemon and examined results with computer models using 'live' data from the field, and then I used theoretical skills to analyse and evaluate these results. I hope that my fieldwork at school will have helped me prepare for university.

A level IT is helping me use various applications to support my research work in A level geography and biology. I really enjoy biology as, like geography, it is about the evolution, adaptation and development of organisms. Its appeal is that it complements my work on the physical development of the Earth and the human impact upon it.

Completing the Duke of Edinburgh Bronze, Silver and Gold Awards was physically and mentally challenging. Attaining Grade 4 flute, playing in the school orchestra and passing my driving test are some of the varied skills I have enjoyed and acquired. While on the Isle of Arran, I really enjoyed the challenge of studying the environment and how it was shaped by geographical and geological processes.

I am a keen gymnast and I really enjoy sports, in particular tennis, hockey and netball. As part of my community service I qualified as an assistant gymnastics coach. I hope that I can use these skills while at university so that I can be part of the university and the local community.

This year I was elected as school prefect. My subject responsibilities are geography and information and communication technology. As part of my role as a geography prefect, I am currently in the process of developing a Geography Society. This will include arranging debates about current geographical issues and organising other activities such as model making and quizzes. I am also involved in helping host the World Wide Quiz for local schools. Other roles include responsibility for Junior School and being Minute Secretary for meetings for the headmistress and prefects. I am also part of a team involved in the development of a new school prospectus. I have improved my organisation and communication skills through involvement in school events and working closely with the Parents' Committee at social and fundraising events.

I enjoy travelling and last year I went to Russia with an Irish dance school, visiting Moscow and Perm. This trip gave me the chance to see a different culture and landscape as we travelled through the taiga on the Trans-Siberian Express. The isolated rural villages with few resources were especially interesting and memorable. I look forward to studying geography to degree level. I believe I am positive, enthusiastic and able to manage my academic and extra-curricular activities, and feel I am well prepared for the challenge of university life and all that it has to offer.

 # TOP TIPS

1 Ensure your qualifications meet published admissions criteria for the particular degree course for which you are applying before you even start to write your personal statement

2 Provide honest and reflective comments in your personal statement about why you wish to study at university and what you want to achieve and pay attention to presentation (for example, checking for correct spelling and grammar)

 # THINGS TO AVOID

1 Applying for courses without having checked you have the correct qualifications to offer

2 Using literary quotes, or unlikely and apparently deeply thoughtful insights about your degree to try to impress

3 Applying to courses that you do not feel passionate about. The lack of passion is often evident in the personal statement

4 Being careless with the writing of the application, for example, not checking for spelling mistakes, missing information required by the admissions team. Not being professional is a bad sign for any admissions tutor and any future employer

RECOMMENDED READING AND WEBSITES

- *New Scientist*: www.newscientist.com
- *Nature*: www.nature.com
- *Discover*: www.discovermagazine.com
- *National Geographic*: www.nationalgeographic.com
- Royal Geographical Society: www.rgs.org
- Geological Association: www.geologists.org.uk
- Centre for Environment, Fisheries and Aquaculture Science: www.cefas.co.uk
- National Oceanography Centre: www.noc.ac.uk
- Society for Underwater Technology: www.sut.org

I am grateful to the Oceanography Department at the University of Southampton (www.southampton.ac.uk/oes/undergraduate/study.page) for its support in writing this profile. Other highly rated courses can be found at the universities of Bangor, East Anglia, Liverpool and Plymouth.

PERFORMING ARTS

This academic profile was written using information provided by an admissions tutor at Liverpool Institute for the Performing Arts (LIPA). The information is useful to all applicants, but some of the advice is pertinent to LIPA in particular.

SUBJECT OVERVIEW

A degree course in acting not only provides technical training and the building of a secure acting process but also encourages students to think of their work in a broader context and teaches you to plan, prepare, research and adapt, all of which are important for the actor. It is important to point out that degrees in acting and performance are different to drama. Here the emphasis is on training to become an actor. It is, in that sense, a vocational course. Not all graduates go on to a career in acting. Many teach, direct or work in other positions in the arts. Others join careers as diverse as banking and journalism.

LIPA is not a drama school. It is a university. There is a difference, and many drama schools, such as the Royal Academy of Dramatic Art (RADA) or the Guildhall School of Music and Drama in London, offer similar courses. These are often non-UCAS in that you apply to them direct. For more information, look online for drama schools that are non-UCAS.

LIPA, along with other schools, also offers courses in dance, costume design, technical theatre and theatre arts management. LIPA also offers courses in music and sound technology. Do your research carefully.

WHAT SKILLS OR ATTRIBUTES DO ADMISSIONS TUTORS LOOK FOR IN A GOOD APPLICANT?

Academically, most departments are looking for a person with five GCSE passes at a minimum of grade C or above, normally including English and maths. In terms of Level 3 qualifications, LIPA does not specify which subjects you need to study – we are looking for people who achieve a minimum of:

- Grades B and C at A level or AVCE level. All A level subjects accepted, excluding general studies
- Merit, Merit, Pass Profile at BTEC National Diploma level

All equivalent UK and overseas qualifications are also accepted, including Scottish Highers, Welsh, European and International Baccalaureate and Irish Leaving Certificate.

LAMDA or equivalent qualifications are useful to have and should be promoted in the personal statement.

We are interested in your talent and ability as an actor, so a level of experience in acting, preferably in a variety of contexts, is definitely something we look for. We will often call you for interview, which will include an audition. You will need to work on a monologue that you prepare in advance and may be asked to take part in group work. Some universities will suggest audition pieces and others will not.

Your interdisciplinary experience is also important, so we look for your potential to train in a second discipline (for example, directing, singing, dancing).

You do not have to be a polished performer – demonstrable potential is equally important. We are also interested in your communication skills and in people who can demonstrate that they are enterprising.

In terms of personality traits, we also look for people who are hungry to learn and can self-manage their learning. A good sense of humour and the ability to work collaboratively are useful traits for an actor. An ability to articulate that you can reflect on your practical experience – whether orally or in writing – is important.

WHAT DOES A GOOD PERSONAL STATEMENT LOOK LIKE?

The most important thing is to communicate a sense of why you think acting is important. The danger is that you may write this in a way that comes across as egocentric. While a level of passion should be evident, your statement should support this with examples of relevant experience. An ability to look beyond the most obviously available opportunities (such as the school play) is an additional factor that can help make you stand out. Simply to say that you have always wanted to be an actor or always had a dream to act is not enough. In addition, any experience that suggests engagement with broader social issues can be a positive reinforcement (for example, voluntary work, travel, responsible roles within school or other organisations).

Examples from good personal statements

'All the world's a stage' Shakespeare once said, and for me this statement is truer than any other. Drama and performing is my passion, ever since a young age my sights have been set on performing at the highest level. Through the years, my desire to achieve my goals of becoming an actress in the West End and to join the Royal Shakespeare Company have become stronger and more focused. I believe that my acceptance into this, one of the leading conservatoires in Britain – if not the world – will be the best starting stepping-stone into this highly competitive profession.

✓ This opening paragraph in the applicant's personal statement illustrates her passion for a career in acting and demonstrates her focus.

I am a member of several different theatre groups and musical theatre companies, doing around three public performances locally every year, plus musical reviews regularly for local charity events and private functions. My membership in one of these groups recently afforded me the invaluable experience of performing in the National Theatre, London, as part of the Youth Theatre Shell Connections Festival. Therefore, I feel that my performance experience is definitely a strong point. I have also done professional work.

✓ This paragraph demonstrates that the applicant has experience in a range of contexts and has an understanding of the differences involved in acting in different contexts. She has been doing reviews for local charity events and private functions, which suggests enterprise. And we can only agree with her statement 'Therefore I feel that my performance experience is definitely a strong point'. She has clearly made the effort to get herself involved with a lot of acting activities.

As well as a great interest in drama/theatre and musicals, I am a keen sportswoman, achieving a place in the Welsh development netball squad in 2014, and I have a strong interest in dance and movement, also attaining a trained level of stage combat and movement. Other interests that I have include art, languages, reading and singing. As a musician, I have also achieved Grade 5 singing, Grade 5 in flute and in violin Grade 3. I also have a keen interest in composing and being a lyricist.

✓ This final paragraph demonstrates that the applicant is trainable in more than one discipline (movement and music). She also engages in other forms of social activity, outside of the performing arts, as she identifies her achievements in netball. Stage combat is also relevant to the acting course. Her interest in art, languages and reading suggest an all-round general sense of enquiry about the world.

Another candidate says:

> Being a member of two drama companies for five years gave me the experience to broaden my horizons. After this I acquired a taste for the stage and knew I wanted to perform professionally on the West End. I went on to further my performing experience in the world of film by working for three years as an extra and had small parts with Mersey Television. Also, playing a main role in a short film for trainee purposes helped me improve my skills in front of the camera.

✓ This shows a good breadth of acting experience and also enterprise. The applicant is clearly committed because he has sought out these acting opportunities.

> Working part-time behind the bar at my local sports and social club, and weekends at my local supermarket has improved my communication and social skills, which enables me to interact well with others.

✓ This suggests he is good at managing his time. He must be self-disciplined to manage to fit this work in, on top of his studies. It's also good that he has perceived the benefits of improving his communication and social skills.

> I am looking forward to focusing on all aspects of the performing arts in more depth, facing new challenges and meeting different people throughout my time at university. I hope to further acquire a variety of skills that will benefit me in life and in my chosen career.

✓ This last paragraph shows his focus and suitability for our course, plus a hunger to learn and recognition of the benefits that come from meeting different people.

 TOP TIPS

The following advice comes in part from a recent LIPA graduate. The advice is good for anyone applying to study acting at any of the major schools, although she studies with us here at LIPA

1 See as much theatre or performance art as possible. Watching with an interested and critical eye helps you in so many ways. If you can look at others with a critical eye, you can also look at

 TOP TIPS FOR AUDITIONS

1 Make sure you understand every word of any chosen piece and do not pick these from an 'audition speeches' book

2 Always read around before picking audition speeches and songs

3 Be prepared to talk about anything that you may have mentioned in your personal statement

yourself in the same way. Make sure you mention your recent experience in your statement

2 You must be certain that the course you choose to apply for is right for you. Be thorough in your research of the course and institution. You need to do everything you can to be confident in your choices. This confidence in the course should be obvious in your statement – tell the tutor that you have done the right research and know that this is the right course for you

3 Sell your achievements in a positive way – do not undersell yourself, and where you can, mention any performance, production, directing or other relevant experience

4 Dress appropriately – you need to see any audition as a practical job interview, so dress appropriately – do not dress in an outfit you would wear for social occasions

 THINGS TO AVOID

1 Leaving preparation to the last minute – you will not be able to learn that Shakespeare speech on the train to LIPA or any other acting school

2 Careless errors in your statement

3 Anything that you cannot defend or discuss at interview

4 Copying from another source

 RECOMMENDED READING AND WEBSITES

- Alison Hodge, *Actor Training*, London: Routledge, 2010
- Creative and Cultural Skills: www.ccskills.org.uk
- Drama UK: www.dramauk.co.uk

I am grateful to LIPA (www.lipa.ac.uk) for its assistance in writing this profile. Other highly regarded courses can be found at the universities of Middlesex, Roehampton and Edge Hill.

PHILOSOPHY

This academic profile was written by an admissions tutor at King's College London. The information is useful to all applicants, but some of the advice is pertinent to King's in particular.

SUBJECT OVERVIEW

Philosophy is one of the oldest and most fundamental academic disciplines that examines the nature of the universe and humanity's place in it. It explores the essence of mind, language, morality and physical reality, and discusses the methods used to investigate these topics. Studying philosophy at university will give you the chance to get to grips with these themes by reading and discussing what great philosophers have had to say about them and forming your own ideas, at the same time developing your powers of logical and creative thinking.

Many departments offer philosophy as a single honours degree together with a range of courses that offer philosophy as a second subject as part of a joint honours course. The options are huge. Kings offers philosophy with, among other things, theology, English, maths, history, modern languages and physics. There is a reasonable mathematics component in the average single honours philosophy degree course. As a result you would need to take care to choose a course that best suits your skills.

A standard philosophy course will include modules on ethics, philosophy of religion, epistemology, logic and political philosophy.

Entry requirements vary depending on the prestige of the university. The standard entry for King's is high (AAA or the equivalent). There are many other good courses out there with lower entry standards. It is not uncommon for the admissions tutor to want to see that your maths is up to scratch. King's does not expect any particular subject but would like to see an A in GCSE Maths.

Career prospects are good as many of the skills you learn (concise writing, debating, analysis and critical thinking) are very transferable into the workplace. Good students end up working in all professions, including the law, teaching, civil service, banking, accountancy and the media.

WHAT SKILLS OR ATTRIBUTES DO ADMISSIONS TUTORS LOOK FOR IN A GOOD APPLICANT?

We are looking for students who enjoy thinking about fundamental questions in a logical way. The ability to express yourself clearly both orally and in writing is important. Students who do well at philosophy tend to be open minded and able to take and receive criticism freely but fairly. Since philosophy rarely reaches definitive answers to the questions it poses, a sense of curiosity is vital, but patience can also be a useful attribute.

You do not have to study philosophy formally at school, although we do like to see some evidence of your interest in the subject. This could be shown through reading that you have done and mentioned in the personal statement or an activity that you have undertaken that shows an interest in debate. We would recommend that you read at least one or two of the many good introductions to philosophy that you will find in any good bookshop or library. Once you have read the introduction, try to read about a particular branch that interests you – perhaps moral philosophy, political philosophy or aesthetics.

Competition for entry is high in many of the best departments. Do your research well to find the best fit for you.

WHAT DOES A GOOD PERSONAL STATEMENT LOOK LIKE?

The most important thing is that you tell us clearly why you want to study philosophy at university and show us some evidence of your interest in the subject. We need to see some evidence of this in your reading so far. You do not need to have read all the major works or even to be particularly expert in any.

However, we would hope to see evidence that you have read one of the better general introductions to the subject and one of the more accessible philosophers' works. Plato's *Republic* is a good introductory text, as is Mill's *Utilitarianism*.

We hope to read a statement that is clear, concise and precise in its presentation. Philosophy is, after all, a subject that is essentially transmitted orally and on paper. If you are applying for a joint honours degree that is fine, as long as we can read about both subjects in your statement.

We are predominantly interested in your academic profile but also keen to hear about your extra-curricular pursuits.

 TOP TIPS

1 Write about why you are interested in studying philosophy. This should be an obvious point, but a significant number of applicants, particularly those

 THINGS TO AVOID

1 Supplying lots of unnecessary detail about your hobbies and travel abroad – although foreign travel might be more relevant to applications for

applying for joint degrees, say nothing or very little about why they want to do philosophy

2 Mention a few books on philosophy that you have read, and what you found of value in them. Do not just give a reading list

3 If you are also applying for other subjects, feel free to say so, but don't neglect the first two tips!

4 Break your statement up into sections (not too many), don't write it as one continuous paragraph

5 Write clearly and grammatically, and avoid spelling errors

6 Make sure that you proofread your statement properly and that it flows well

other subjects, especially modern languages

2 Telling us at length how wonderful you think philosophy is and/or how passionate you are about it – we like to see enthusiasm, but be concise and specific rather than vague and general

3 Using jargon and technical vocabulary that you don't understand, just because it sounds impressive – it may impress your friends (though it may not) but it won't fool an experienced university teacher

4 Explaining at length why you want to do a degree other than the one for which you have applied, or at another institution

5 Boasting – let your achievements speak for themselves

6 Plagiarising your personal statement – a serious error of judgement!

 # RECOMMENDED READING AND WEBSITES

- Nigel Warburton, *Philosophy: The Basics*, Routledge, 2012
- Nigel Warburton, *Philosophy: The Classics*, Routledge, 2014
- Simon Blackburn, *Think: A Compelling Introduction to Philosophy*, Oxford University Press, 2001
- Plato, *The Republic*
- Philosophy Bites, www.philosophybites.com – a very good philosophy podcast.

I am grateful to the Philosophy Department at King's College London (www.kcl.ac.uk) for its support in compiling this profile. Other highly rated courses can be found at the universities of Oxford, Cambridge, St Andrews, the London School of Economics and Stirling.

PHYSICS

This academic profile was written by an admissions tutor at the University of Bath and focuses on physics as a single honours discipline. The information is useful to all applicants, but please be aware that some of the advice may be pertinent to Bath in particular.

SUBJECT OVERVIEW

Physics is a fundamental science; it is concerned with the study of matter, energy and the interactions between them, and it involves the search for the universal principles underlying many and diverse natural phenomena. It is important not only as a subject in its own right but also as an essential element in all the other natural sciences, engineering and technology. There is also a great deal of enjoyment and satisfaction to be derived from an understanding of the most recent developments in physics research.

Physics graduates combine sound mathematical, theoretical and experimental expertise with the ability to grasp new concepts and are able to apply their expertise to many familiar and unfamiliar challenges. Physics often involves the development of mathematical models of complex behaviour and develops the judgement and imagination necessary to solve problems at an appropriate level of approximation. The development of many other important skills – such as written and verbal communication, computational skills and team-working – is embedded in physics degree programmes.

The versatility of physicists is reflected in the wide variety of occupations in which they may be found. Nearly all modern industries call on the insight and technical expertise of physics graduates. Physicists are equally valued for the contribution they can make to education, administration, business and commerce, where their analytical and problem-solving skills are in great demand.

WHAT SKILLS OR ATTRIBUTES DO ADMISSIONS TUTORS LOOK FOR IN A GOOD APPLICANT?

The most important attributes are a high level of competence in mathematics and physics, with particular emphasis on the latter, an interest in problem solving and an enthusiasm for the study of physics. Admissions tutors also look for good communication skills and evidence of ability to work alone or in groups. However, most students exhibit a tremendous diversity of personalities and interests, and we are very pleased that this is the case.

WHAT DOES A GOOD PERSONAL STATEMENT LOOK LIKE?

Your statement is going to be read by five admissions tutors from five different departments – so avoid being too specific in stating your interests – for example, not every department offers biophysics options; do not betray your first choice(s); do not say that you have always wanted to be a mathematician if you are applying for both mathematics and physics programmes, or even for joint degree programmes. If you are applying to physics programmes as an alternative to a medical degree, then make this clear in your statement (for example, do not just mention medicine).

We look for good grammatical construction and good motivation. Don't just write what you think you should, and definitely don't download. Be original without being quirky for the sake of it. Anything you write about is fair game for discussion if you are interviewed, when you will be expected to be able to talk about anything in your statement – so be honest.

At Bath, in common with most other physics departments in the country, we pay most attention to academic achievement and potential as contained primarily in A level grades (or equivalent). We need to see evidence of the prerequisite knowledge in mathematics and physics to succeed on a challenging programme of study.

We rarely reject a student because of a personal statement; in our experience, most statements are written adequately. Any statement written following the guidelines above would be acceptable. However, in the case of a student who has narrowly missed their offer grades, if we have a few final places to fill, we may look to your statement for signs of something special to differentiate you from someone with identical near-miss grades.

Example of a good personal statement

Students generally begin by expressing their interest in and commitment to physics as a discipline, providing some evidence of this – usually in the form of reading matter and short events they have attended – and end with a description of their other activities and interests. Such statements are fine, but generally contain nothing to catch the eye. The following example is good because it is brief, honest and to the point.

> I have chosen to study physics at university as I want to study a subject that is not only universally useful but is always crossing new frontiers of knowledge.

✓ A good start, and not too flowery. New frontiers of knowledge – cliché alert!

> I particularly want to continue with it as studying the subject over the years has brought just as many new questions to me as it has answered. I have always tried to keep up to date with scientific developments and as such I read issues of 'New Scientist' and I am currently reading the Richard Feynman lectures.

✓ This is good because it avoids the obvious reference to Stephen Hawking or Brian Cox! Many people may read the Feynman lectures, but did you understand them? It's nice to see an insightful statement derived from the reading. What did this extra reading teach you?

> In July 2013, I attended a three-day physics course at ... University.

✓ Excellent. But did you participate or just attend?

> This was a valuable experience, involving problem-solving exercises and sample lectures, which gave me an insight into the areas of physics in which I would be most interested in specialising. Nanoscience is an area that consequently attracted me due to its interdisciplinary nature, as it can be applied to practically everything, from electronics to engineering, to biology and the environment. I'm sure there will be great progress in this field in the near future.
>
> I have applied for MPhys/MSci courses as I am keen to pursue a career in research, and as such my shortlist of universities have all been selected for their strong research facilities.

✓ Shows that some research has been done into which choices to make and there's some awareness of what the day-to-day experience of the course will be.

> Aside from mathematics and physics, I also chose my A levels to cater for analytical skills and to keep up a well-rounded education. Classics was a completely new subject to me and I was interested in taking on something fresh. History provided more breadth to my A levels, and I think it is important to be well informed, particularly on aspects of modern world history. Both of these subjects have the bonus of maintaining my fluency in essay writing.

✓ Evidence of scholarship.

> I enjoy music and am an avid guitarist. I play acoustic, bass and, in particular, electric to a very high standard. I frequently play with others for entertainment and have posted videos of performance on the internet which received very pleasing feedback. I also write music, and aside from my own compositions I am working on a number of joint projects with a friend. My experience of studying the waves part of the A level Physics syllabus last year has even come in useful in playing the guitar, as I found that I have encountered many phenomena such as resonance and standing waves, and have in fact taken advantage of these for musical effect.

✓ Good. Evidence of interests outside school. Also, it's worth noting that physics clearly isn't as vocational as medicine, veterinary science, architecture or law. So, we don't expect you to have already practised as a scientist in a lab before applying to study physics. However, the MPhys/MSci courses are designed for students who most likely want to proceed to career scientists. It's nice to see evidence of applicants thinking like scientists and applying their physics knowledge to real-world situations – here the physics of musical instruments – rather than just seeing physics as a remote, academic facts list.

In researching courses, I was encouraged to see the large investment currently being made in physics departments, and I am certain there are many interesting developments in which I can become involved.

✓ Shows evidence of research into her chosen universities.

Examples from poor personal statements

The following sentences are taken from the beginnings of statements representing the vast majority we receive, which are unlikely to catch the eye.

Ever since an early age I have been fascinated by physics, in particular how and why things work and how vast the subject of physics is …

Ever since primary school I have been interested in sciences …

Physics has always intrigued me …

My interest in physics was first awakened when I read 'A Brief History of Time' by Stephen Hawking at the age of 13 …

The wonders of earth and space have interested me from an early age …

For many years I have been interested in the sciences …

I was fascinated by science and maths from my first years at secondary school …

From an early age I have wanted to study physics so that I can attempt to understand the universe around me …

When I was a child I always asked, why? I'm now 18 and I still do.

The following are two examples of misdirected statements in applications to read single-subject physics.

I hold a strong desire to study physics and philosophy at university.

Since a very young age, I have had a strong desire to become a doctor.

 TOP TIPS

1 Find out as much about the course as you can so that in your personal statement you can talk about specific elements that interest you, and why

2 Make sure you have good reasons for applying to your chosen courses and explain these in your statement

 THINGS TO AVOID

1 A poorly constructed statement, full of grammatical errors and clichés

2 Writing fanciful prose, especially in the opening sentence

3 Mentioning specialities not relevant to some of your chosen departments

3 Try to be original with your opening statement without being quirky. Admissions tutors have to read hundreds of statements so something more unusual is likely to catch their interest

4 Refer to your A level (or equivalent) courses and demonstrate how these will prepare you for degree-level study of physics

5 Give evidence of other interests and show how these have given you additional skills that will be useful for university-level study

4 Mentioning your top choice(s) – you may change your mind!

5 Saying you have read Stephen Hawking's *A Brief History of Time*. You may well have done (at least partly), and this is commendable, but we read this statement in a large number of our applications and it has become a kind of cliché which does not lift you above the crowd

---

RECOMMENDED READING AND WEBSITES

- Institute of Physics – look particularly at the section for students: www.iop.org/tailored/students
- Institute of Physics and Engineering in Medicine: www.ipem.ac.uk
- Physics World: www.physicsworld.com

I am grateful to the University of Bath (www.bath.ac.uk) for its support in compiling this profile. Other highly rated courses can be found at the universities of Oxford, Birmingham, University College London, Imperial College and Leeds.

PHYSIOTHERAPY

This academic profile was written by an admissions tutor at the University of Brighton. The information in this profile is useful to all applicants, but some of the advice is pertinent to Brighton in particular.

SUBJECT OVERVIEW

Physiotherapy is a healthcare profession concerned with human function and movement. Physiotherapists share in peoples' journeys, improving their quality of life by helping them to maintain or improve their physical abilities through advice, exercise and education. As a physiotherapist you will work closely with a diverse variety of people with physical illnesses caused by accident, injury or that arise from a variety of conditions affecting their health and well-being, and who need individually tailored treatment and attention. To succeed you will need compassion, patience and excellent interpersonal skills.

To ensure you are confident applying theory to clinical practice, you'll spend around 30 weeks on placement in varied settings. You will simulate handling different situations in our practical skills rooms that are fully equipped with professional-standard equipment.

Degree programmes in physiotherapy provide both university experience and the experience of working with people in healthcare settings. The students go into clinical settings to work with qualified physiotherapists and other health professionals, for example, nurses, doctors and occupational therapists. This balance of academic and work-based learning is excellent preparation for a career in healthcare.

All physiotherapy degrees need to carry eligibility for state registration, enabling graduates to practise as physiotherapists and be approved by the professional body, the Chartered Society of Physiotherapists. You will be asked to complete a Disclosure and Barring Service clearance (a police check) to ensure that you are deemed an appropriate person to work with children and vulnerable adults. This is conducted after you accept the offer and you will be charged a fee for it. You will also need to comply with the department's occupational heath guidelines and show that you have up-to-date vaccinations.

Entry requirements vary, but competition is high. Most require an A level in biology or sports science. Some require chemistry. Do check the requirements carefully before you apply. Physiotherapy departments are used to welcoming students with alternative qualifications and mature students.

UK/EU students are funded by the NHS. This means that at present the tuition fees are met by the government. This is correct at the time of publication but may change, so do ensure that you check carefully when applying.

Interviews are common and admissions tutors will expect you to have a good understanding of what a physiotherapist does in the NHS and some awareness of NHS policies. Do read a good newspaper to keep up with changes in NHS policy. You will be surprised how many interviewees have little awareness of issues such as seven-day working in the NHS or funding problems.

WHAT SKILLS OR ATTRIBUTES DO ADMISSIONS TUTORS LOOK FOR IN A GOOD APPLICANT?

We are looking for enthusiastic people who have a good academic profile, from a wide range of educational experiences and who are prepared to learn. We would like to recruit students who are motivated and have made the effort to find out about physiotherapy. We are particularly keen on people who have had the opportunity to observe different aspects of physiotherapy and are able to explain why they are interested in developing a career in the area.

We do expect candidates to have undertaken some work experience and to have spent some time shadowing a physiotherapist. This is best done at a local hospital. In the first instance, contact the human resources department of your local hospital. You can also show an interest in people by working in a care environment as a volunteer. This could be in an old peoples' home, with children or in a hospice.

Please do not emphasise an interest in sports physiotherapy. This shows a lack of awareness of life for the average physiotherapist. You may well become the Arsenal physio, but you will need to have worked in the NHS for a while first!

WHAT DOES A GOOD PERSONAL STATEMENT LOOK LIKE?

It is really helpful, if you have observed some physiotherapy sessions, to briefly describe your experience and explain why you would like to study physiotherapy. You really need to describe something more varied than a personal experience of receiving physiotherapy, which shows that you have made an effort to see different aspects of physiotherapy – or at least have plans to broaden your understanding. Many departments do not look favourably at an overemphasis on sport. Most physiotherapists work in hospital settings and do not get involved in any form of sports-related injury or rehabilitation.

It is always good to hear about your activities beyond the academic, particularly if you are interested in continuing them at university. If you can, try to show a range of interests other than sport. We are interested in music, drama and other extra-curricular pursuits, especially if they show evidence of individual leadership or team-work skills. If you have had a job or done voluntary work make sure that you explain something positive about the experience of interacting with people.

Try to find a balance between self-promotion, explaining your recent experiences of work, social activities and school achievements. Over-emphasis on any of these elements can skew your statement.

Example of a good personal statement

I have shadowed a sports physiotherapist and spent time in an NHS hospital, where I shadowed both junior and senior physiotherapists in all wards; this, combined with my own personal research of the career by means of literature and talking with many physiotherapists, has served to increase my desire to commit myself to a career as a physiotherapist.

✓ Shows that an effort has been made beyond personal experience and that active research has been done to understand physiotherapy.

The diversity in the roles astounded me, ranging from the intricacies of the hand clinic to the very manual rehabilitation of stroke patients, where constant feedback on posture and walking gait is given. Despite the various techniques employed, several competencies became very evident to me: a physiotherapist is an excellent communicator, a problem-solving team player who can work holistically with other members of a multidisciplinary team whose goals are to educate and rehabilitate a patient so that they may return to everyday life as speedily as possible.

✓ Shows some well-informed opinion.

Having travelled and met people from many different backgrounds and age groups, I am confident that I now possess the maturity and keenness of mind to undertake a physiotherapy degree and meet with enthusiasm any of the challenges that a career as a Chartered Physiotherapist poses.

✓ A very literate statement; could also include more personal information about hobbies.

 TOP TIPS

1 Indicate early on your passion for the subject, with examples to support this interest

2 Show that you are interested in current health issues

3 Tell the tutor about your work experience and contact with physiotherapists. Say what you learnt from this experience and how it helped you to make up your mind to apply

4 Make sure that your science skills are clearly developed in your personal statement

 THINGS TO AVOID

1 Telling us how much you want to be a nurse/doctor/work in the leisure industry

2 Writing about anything you are not prepared to talk about at interview

3 Writing about sport to the exclusion of all else – many departments do not look favourably at an over-emphasis on sport. Most physiotherapists work in hospital settings and do not get involved in any form of sports-related rehabilitation

4 Confusing physiotherapy and psychotherapy!

5 Write a list of things you have done – be specific and pick out the best

6 It is always good to hear about your activities beyond the academic, particularly if you are interested in continuing them at university

7 Try to find a balance between self-promotion, explaining your recent experiences of work, social activities and school achievements. Over-emphasis on any of these elements can skew your statement

5 Poor spelling, punctuation and grammar – get your statement proofread by a competent teacher or tutor

RECOMMENDED READING AND WEBSITES

Reading any current affairs information about health issues and physiotherapy would be good but there are no particular activities other than your natural keenness to pursue a career in physiotherapy. It would make sense to read a book about what it is like to be a physiotherapist; there are a variety on the market that bring the subject to life. The Chartered Society of Physiotherapists has a good website with a range of information that would extend your knowledge of the subject.

- James Barton, *Getting into Physiotherapy Courses*, Trotman Education, 2016
- The Chartered Society of Physiotherapists: www.csp.org.uk
- Health and Care Professions Council: www.hpc-uk.org

I am grateful to the University of Brighton (www.brighton.ac.uk) for its support in preparing this profile. Other highly rated courses can be found at the universities of Birmingham, King's College London, West of England (UWE), Southampton and St George's Hospital, London.

PODIATRY

This academic profile was written by an admissions tutor at the University of Brighton. The information is useful to all applicants, but some of the advice is pertinent to Brighton in particular.

SUBJECT OVERVIEW

Podiatrists (previously known as chiropodists) diagnose and treat abnormalities of the lower limb. They give professional advice on the prevention of foot problems, and on proper care of the foot. Patients will be of all ages, from infants to the elderly. Working as a podiatrist can be exciting and rewarding because it involves working in a variety of environments with a number of other healthcare professionals and many different groups of patients who have a wide range of podiatric problems.

The scope of practice of a podiatrist is often much wider than many people realise. Some examples of this are the following:

- Children sometimes have pains in their legs or feet as they grow or have problems walking.
- People with diabetes may have problems with their circulation or sensation in their feet.
- Sportsmen and sportswomen often suffer from injuries to their legs and feet.
- Dancers with long hours of rehearsing and performing put stress through their feet that can cause injury.
- Some people may need minor surgery, such as nail surgery or laser treatment.
- Some people may want advice about footwear or foot health.

To become a practitioner registered by the Health and Care Professions Council, there is a requirement to undertake and pass a three-year full-time honours degree in podiatry. The degree also provides eligibility to apply for membership of the College of Podiatry (www.scpod.org).

In addition to the in-house clinical placement occurring every week during the semesters, the course at the University of Brighton (along with others in the UK) includes a minimum of six further weeks of external clinical placement with NHS trusts. Students benefit from the multidisciplinary medical team, specialist hospital ward rounds, outpatient clinics and orthopaedic operating sessions. Short placements are arranged with specialist podiatrists and a variety of allied health professionals so that the student experiences as wide a range of podiatric care as possible.

The podiatry undergraduate programme is very intensive and requires considerable dedication on the part of the student.

WHAT SKILLS OR ATTRIBUTES DO ADMISSIONS TUTORS LOOK FOR IN A GOOD APPLICANT?

The normal minimum entrance requirements are GCSE C or above in five subjects including English, mathematics and science, with an additional expectation that the student will obtain a BBC in A levels, to include a science, or DDM at a BTEC, to include a science subject. Mature students enter the programme by a variety of routes, the most common being approved standard Access to Higher Education Diploma and prior degree qualifications. Entrance requirements may differ for courses at other universities.

You should be well motivated to learn and have enthusiasm to study at degree level. You should also be fully committed to this area of work.

Communication is probably the most important skill a healthcare worker should possess. You should be able to communicate effectively both orally and in writing. Although you will be helped to develop these skills during the course of your degree, having well-developed interpersonal skills will help you in both the practice learning and theoretical aspects of this programme.

The administration of local anaesthesia and the appreciation of mechanics and statistics in podiatry mean that an understanding of mathematics is required to GCSE grade B level.

Computer technology is used extensively in healthcare and it is therefore important that your ICT skills are developed. Basic word processing, spreadsheet and internet search skills are therefore essential on enrolment, while you can develop others, such as PowerPoint, during the programme.

WHAT DOES A GOOD PERSONAL STATEMENT LOOK LIKE?

Motivation and commitment: podiatry is a fascinating subject and a stimulating profession and practitioners are privileged to have working relationships with some of the most vulnerable members of society. You should show an appreciation of the scope of podiatry and the role of the podiatrist within the multidisciplinary healthcare team, and you should be able to indicate that you are fully committed to this area of work.

Interpersonal skills: as communication is probably the most important skill a healthcare worker should possess, you will need to consider how you have demonstrated effective communication in your life. Ideally this will be communication to a mixed audience, using a variety of methods and perhaps even at different levels.

Caring and compassion: you should demonstrate caring skills through discussion of work or life experiences. A compassionate nature is an essential criterion for admission onto this course.

Interest in working and learning as part of a team: admissions tutors will be looking for skills of working with others towards a shared goal and operating as part of a team. After-school activities such as debating societies and membership of sports teams can be used as examples of this. Other evidence can be drawn from appropriate discussion of previous life experiences.

Manual dexterity skills: practical podiatry requires a high level of dexterity. Your application should mention your acquisition of manual dexterity skills, for example the practice of art and craft skills, playing a musical instrument, design and technology skills.

Example of a good personal statement

The following applicant demonstrated all the qualities our admissions team look for both by the written word and by using specific examples. Her statement was logical in presentation, well written and with a wide vocabulary, and gave consideration to the attributes a healthcare worker should possess.

> **I have always been captivated by the human body and how it can perform the most complex of tasks without conscious thought. Because of this fascination, I chose to study human biology and psychology at A2 level, as well as sports studies at AS. Through these subjects I have been able to learn more about the mechanics of the body and the relationship of body and mind.**

✓ She has attempted to link human physiology with the working of the brain, demonstrating an appreciation that podiatry is about psychosocial issues, not just biology.

> **Having always aspired to a career in healthcare, I have decided to pursue a degree in podiatry. Having researched the subject thoroughly, I find the scope of opportunities within the profession very exciting.**

✓ This shows she has actively looked for information, particularly career choices.

> **Biomechanics is an area that fascinates me. Having enjoyed the academic study of anatomy and physiology in my A levels, I am eager to combine this theory with practical applications.**

✓ This shows an appreciation that textbook biology needs translating into applied practice.

> **I am also keen to learn more about the surgical aspect of podiatry. I have had the opportunity to take part in a weekly work experience placement at a podiatry clinic. Through this, I have been able to gain an invaluable insight into the profession in a clinical environment. I am learning at first hand about the practical and theoretical side of podiatry, which has further confirmed my desire to study this subject.**

✓ This demonstrates motivation and commitment, and that she has been exposed to a reasonable scope of podiatric practice.

> **Outside school, I have worked in retail. From this, I have gained experience in the real world, undertaking responsibilities and learning to work with a wide range of people. I enjoy meeting and talking with customers, establishing their needs and having the satisfaction of being able to help them. I have won two awards for my customer service skills.**

✓ Communication skills are evidenced here, along with the appreciation that healthcare offers a service to a wide audience. She also illustrates her sense of responsibility.

> **Working with other employees in a team has hugely improved my communication skills, but I also enjoy the challenges of using my own initiative. This has greatly improved my self-confidence.**

✓ Podiatrists work as part of a team, but for much of their practice they have to work in single-chair clinics. This applicant is demonstrating an understanding of the importance of both modes of working.

> **My elderly grandmother lives with me in the family home. I often sit and chat with her at mealtimes to keep her company while she eats, and I help her take her medications if she is getting a little muddled.**

✓ This is demonstrating a caring attitude towards a relative, and the understanding that nutrition is important to maintain good health. It also alludes to a compassionate nature by assisting someone who may be showing signs of forgetfulness to carry out their everyday activities.

> **My interest in human biology drove me to learn first aid. I am now a fully trained volunteer first aider and cadet leader with St John Ambulance. I devote most of my spare time to organising cadet activities and providing first-aid cover at local events. Due to the nature of the work I have to communicate effectively and sensitively with a cross-section of people, often in highly stressful situations. I love the work I do, and get great satisfaction from being involved in something so rewarding.**

✓ Here she is not only evidencing her skills in caring, but her ability to deal with accidents and events that could involve blood and other traumatic situations. She is also communicating that she has a sense of moral obligation and a strong work ethic, that she can cope with stress, has energy and can organise herself and other people.

> **I can play the piano and have recently taken my Grade 8. In my spare time, I like to listen to music and read novels. Jane Eyre is a particular favourite of mine.**

✓ Manual dexterity skills are shown here, along with a rounded approach to life.

> **From the experiences I have gained, I believe that podiatry is not only the subject I will thoroughly enjoy studying, but that it will provide me with a rewarding long-term career.**

TOP TIPS

1 Your enthusiasm for the subject should be clear in the opening paragraph. Think about ways in which this enthusiasm can be transmitted. If at all possible, arrange to meet a practising podiatrist and include what you learnt from this meeting in your statement – this will give you a real edge

2 The tutors expect to see a well-written statement that shows off your ability to communicate well. Elsewhere, they need to see evidence of your ability to work in teams and communicate effectively to others orally

3 An engaging personality and a caring, compassionate nature should come across in your statement, and later at interview

4 Manual dexterity is a vital part of the assessment process. Any evidence you can provide of an ability to use your hands to make, repair or design will be welcome

5 Show that you have a rounded approach to life, including studies – tell tutors about your interests, particularly those that include a need for independence, initiative and team-work

 THINGS TO AVOID

1 Not being sure what podiatry is – before you apply, make sure that you read up about the subject – indicate this level of research in your statement

2 Mumbling at interview

3 Failing to support or develop points made in your statement at interview

4 Poor spelling, punctuation and grammar

5 A statement that is uninspiring, and lacking in detail about your skills and desire to study this particular vocation

 RECOMMENDED READING AND WEBSITES

- Eric Shi, *Podiatry Student Handbook*, CreateSpace Independent Publishing Platform, 2015
- College of Podiatry: www.scpod.org
- Careers advice for anyone considering podiatry: www.careersinpodiatry.com

I am grateful to the University of Brighton for its assistance in compiling this profile. Other highly rated courses can be found at the universities of Glasgow Caledonian, Huddersfield, Southampton and Ulster.

PSYCHOLOGY

This academic profile was written by an admissions tutor at the University of Nottingham. The information is useful to all applicants, but some of the advice is pertinent to Nottingham in particular.

Most UK courses are accredited by the British Psychological Society and, as such, they are a fine way of preparing for a career as a practising psychologist.

SUBJECT OVERVIEW

Psychology is the scientific study of mental life and human behaviour. It helps to explain how we think, feel and act both individually and as part of a social group. When studying the subject at university you will use a variety of scientific research principles and studies including experiments, brain imaging, interviews, case studies and observations.

Psychology is a broad discipline that covers a number of topics, such as memory, personality, child development, mental illness and social relationships.

A degree in psychology, as well as being extremely interesting, provides a very wide range of employment prospects to its graduates. Modern psychology is a genuine science in its infancy, trying to understand one of the most fascinating systems ever – the human mind. It is a little like studying physics in the days when gravity was just being understood; the field is changing all the time and is rich with new questions to be answered.

Many students (including those who have taken the subject at A level) are surprised about how much of a modern psychology degree concerns experiments testing rigorous hypotheses and studies of brain processes, but they usually learn to appreciate the need for solid, data-based theories.

For this reason, many departments will expect an applicant to have a sound grasp of either biology or chemistry. Do look at this carefully. As a rule of thumb, BA courses normally expect less science and maths. The maths element is mostly statistics and few, if any, expect A level Maths.

Note: if you wish to become a practising psychologist in the NHS or private practice, you will need to complete further study. A clinical psychologist holds a doctorate (PhD) and a child psychologist has normally worked in a school or college before doing the further training.

That being said, the skills you learn on a course do transfer well to other careers and psychologists are often employed in, among others, commerce, human resources, media, marketing, public relations and teaching.

WHAT SKILLS OR ATTRIBUTES DO ADMISSIONS TUTORS LOOK FOR IN A GOOD APPLICANT?

As psychology is a multidisciplinary subject, few subject-specific skills are required to make a good candidate, other than logical reasoning and the ability to learn. Some students come from pure arts backgrounds and really excel at the essay writing; some come from pure science and are very strong in the experimental and analytical components; and some have multidisciplinary backgrounds. We find that any combination can work very well.

We do normally expect candidates' subjects to be broadly academic – psychology is no soft option at university level and we do want to know that students have developed some of the above skills during their sixth-form period.

Entry standards vary hugely and depend on the prestige of the department and name of the university. There are many courses out there, so choose carefully. Some courses are stand-alone, but many are joint honours courses. These are great, but please ensure that you have the skill set that suits both and that the course is accredited by the British Psychological Society if you think that you may wish to pursue a career in psychology.

In terms of personality, the best students are usually just dedicated and keen. Students who can focus their minds on the task at hand and push themselves will do well. Often that comes down to the fact that they find the subject interesting and are more willing to work hard at it. Psychology students are often outgoing and dynamic but these personal attributes are certainly not necessary for successful selection.

University life is very different from school. There is a much bigger drive to encourage 'autonomous learning' in students, fostering their ability to explore topics themselves. Formal teaching is often in much larger groups – lectures may have several hundred students – and is aimed more at providing the initial basis for the students' learning rather than providing the entire syllabus.

Some universities still talk about 'reading for a degree', reflecting the greater amount of time spent in the library than in class.

WHAT DOES A GOOD PERSONAL STATEMENT LOOK LIKE?

Think about your target audience – the admissions tutor. That person's job is to try to work out whether or not you will perform well on his/her course.

You need to show that (a) you know a little about the subject and (b) you really want to study it. These are good indicators of your dedication to the course, because if you enjoy the material you will be keener to work on it. You might show this in different ways; you might want to explain why you are interested in the course if there is some compelling reason that you have always been fascinated by the discipline. You might be able to use evidence of additional work or reading that you have carried out in the topic or demonstrate your knowledge of the subject. Obviously, either of these routes should refer to real aspects of contemporary psychology. Reading a psychology journal or a good book about psychology will stand you in good stead.

One problem for the admissions tutor is trying to work out how generous you are being with the truth. According to most personal statements and references, students are all confident, independent, sociable, intellectual types with excellent debating skills. In reality, some students are terrified, some are not very keen to question and some are at university because they didn't want to get a job yet. The difficulty can be to work out which students are which. You can help here by showing your skills rather than explaining them. Some students will tell us that they subscribe to *Psychological Bulletin*, but others will discuss a psychological issue that they find interesting. By discussing the issue accurately they demonstrate their interest in a way that is harder to fake, which saves the admissions tutor worrying whether or not it is a lie.

Extra-curricular activities may help to show your ability to achieve your goals and your ability to manage your time (if combined with good grades), but do not go overboard. In particular, do not spend a great deal of time describing pastimes that are not likely to make you a better student. At the end of the day, an admissions tutor will be more interested in how well you get through the course than in your love of film or your social charisma. We also want to see a wide variety of personalities. Imagine a department where everyone was gregarious and confident – it would be painful!

Also bear in mind that the way you write your statement is going to be direct evidence for the admissions tutor of how well you write. Make sure your statement is clear, expressive and accurate. Read through it several times and get someone else to read it. If your personal statement is littered with errors an admissions tutor will not believe the reference when it discusses your excellent essay-writing skills.

Your personal statement is also a time to discuss anything unusual about your qualifications so far. We may be interested in students whose grades haven't previously been as good as expected if they have a convincing explanation that this will change. Some students thrive at university, while others suffer from the independent style of learning. Dedication to the course goes a long way. Also, students who have chosen unusual, or less academic, subjects can use this space to explain what the subject is or how it has been beneficial to them in preparing for a psychology degree. Bear in mind that a university lecturer might not realise how much essay writing you had to do, or how much maths is involved in your particular course. The basic skills you develop in the sixth form are at least as useful as the specific knowledge you have, so English and maths are likely to be at least as useful subjects to take as psychology itself.

Example of a good personal statement

The following student was taking history, music and biology A levels as well as general studies and an AS in French. Although she has never studied psychology formally, she demonstrates her enthusiasm for the subject throughout her personal statement and shows a great deal of energy in both her work and extra-curricular pursuits. The statement is written clearly and carefully in appropriate and error-free language. We can have little doubt that the candidate possesses the necessary academic skills, as well as work ethic, to progress very well at university.

> Psychology strikes me as the most fascinating area of study imaginable. I love the fact that it is such a diverse subject, ranging from animal behaviour or inter-group relations to child psychology and research methodology. I am particularly intrigued by developmental psychology, especially abnormal psychology in children, and I am keen to learn more about the ways in which an application of this subject can benefit children with conditions such as autism.

✓ This shows understanding of what a diverse range of subjects modern psychology covers.

> Through my work as a volunteer with special needs children on summer schemes I have begun to understand more about how autistic children discover and learn, and also how a response to their need for solitude, repetition and a strict routine can often bring them great comfort. I have started to learn sign language and other forms of non-verbal communication, such as PECS [Picture Exchange Communication System], to use in stressful situations where speech may be ineffective. In addition, this work has enabled me to develop my ability to take responsibility, often in demanding situations, and to adapt quickly to difficult circumstances, such as relating to a child whose only form of communication is through spitting. I also enjoyed taking sole care of severely disabled children both in hydrotherapy pools and in a sensory room. I have read a number of books, including 'The Man Who Mistook his Wife for a Hat' (Oliver Sachs), and have found 'Abnormal Psychology' (Davison and Neal) useful for reference. I particularly like Margaret Donaldson's 'Children's Minds' as I found Donaldson's criticism of Piaget's theories interesting. Through researching different developmental disorders I was able to gain a better understanding of the individual needs of the children with whom I worked.
>
> I enjoy reading about current issues in psychology, for example the latest ideas on the 'nature versus nature' debate. This is reflected in my A level choices of biology, which I feel

represents the neurological reasons for actions, and history, which shows how past experiences influence decisions and behaviours.

✓ Explaining your choices of A level subjects is good. Actually, this candidate might have done better to emphasise the skills developed during these courses (in history she will have developed her written fluency) rather than pointing out specific information that has been learnt (that behaviour is shaped by previous experience). The skills will be more useful and take much longer to develop.

 ## TOP TIPS

1 Show that (a) you know a little about the subject and (b) you really want to study it. These are good indicators of your dedication to the course, because if you enjoy the material you are keener to work on more difficult aspects

2 Look at exactly what is taught in the department you are applying to and make sure that you indicate somewhere in your statement that you have done this important research

3 Check your form and statement carefully for errors – get your statement proofread by someone you trust

4 Show your skills rather than explain them. Some students will tell us they subscribe to *Psychological Bulletin*, but others will discuss a psychological issue that they find interesting. By discussing the issue accurately they demonstrate their interest in a way that is harder to fake, which saves the admissions tutor worrying whether or not it is a lie

 ## THINGS TO AVOID

1 Discussing, at length, extra-curricular activities that do not make you a better student. Stick to the activities that add value to your application in your statement – don't just list them!

2 Claiming to be widely read on the subject if you actually know little about it – this is often clear when reading the statement and will become clearer if you are called for interview

3 Forgetting for whom you are writing your statement – an admissions tutor (generally a lecturer in the department)

4 Using slang, text-speak or off-the-wall humour

 # RECOMMENDED READING AND WEBSITES

- John Cooter, *Getting into Psychology Courses*, Trotman Education, 2016
- Tanya Bryon, *The Skeleton Cupboard*, Pan, 2015 – a very good introduction to life as a junior clinical psychologist
- Any good introduction to psychology – there are many out there!

- British Association for Counselling and Psychotherapy: www.bacp.co.uk
- Health and Care Professions Council: www.hpc-uk.org
- Occupational Psychology Services: www.opsltd.com
- Association of Educational Psychologists: www.aep.org.uk)
- Division of Forensic Psychologists: www.bps.org.uk/dfp

I am grateful for the support I received from the Psychology Department at the University of Nottingham (www.nottingham.ac.uk) in the preparation of this profile. Other highly rated courses include those at the universities of Oxford, University College London, St Andrews, Royal Holloway and Bristol.

SPORTS AND EXERCISE SCIENCE

This profile was written using information provided by an admissions tutor for Sports and Exercise Science at the University of Essex, but much of the advice here is also relevant to other degree courses involving sport such as sports studies, sports development, sport therapy and coaching science. Please be aware that some of what follows may be particular to Essex.

SUBJECT OVERVIEW

Sports and exercise science is a multidisciplinary subject that covers the physiology, biomechanics and psychology of sport, exercise and physical activity. Students learn how the body responds and adapts to exercise, how and why different energy systems are deployed at different exercise intensities, how the principles of mechanics determine the movement of athletes and objects, how exercise reduces the risk of ill-health and how mind and body interact to influence performance. In short, studying sports and exercise science gives students a new perspective on the world of sport, exercise, health and physical fitness.

WHAT SKILLS OR ATTRIBUTES DO ADMISSIONS TUTORS LOOK FOR IN A GOOD APPLICANT?

Desirable academic skills include good oral and written communication, team-work and some evidence of practical scientific skill. Students on sport-related courses generally have a great personal interest in sport and exercise and tend to participate in sport-related activities in their personal lives. However, excellence in sport is not necessary.

The A level requirements vary between institutions. Admissions tutors will often expect at least one science at A2 (or equivalent), such as biology, physical education, maths, chemistry or psychology.

WHAT DOES A GOOD PERSONAL STATEMENT LOOK LIKE?

Demonstrate your knowledge and enthusiasm, both for sports science as an academic discipline and for sport in general. You may want to research the courses you are applying for, as sport-related courses can vary in content across institutions. Focus on a couple of aspects that all your chosen courses have in common – such as anatomy or sports psychology. You may want to mention anything you are currently studying that has inspired you to pursue sport science at a higher level. It is certainly a good idea to talk about your extra-curricular activities relating to sport and any positions of responsibility these have led to. Highlight if you are keen to continue your involvement when you are at university. However, it is important to focus on your interest in the degree and why it is your chosen course.

Example of a personal statement

I have always wanted a career in sport. Since taking A level Sports Science my eyes have been opened to the opportunities that are available at undergraduate level. Detailed research has confirmed that a degree in sports science will provide me with a solid understanding of the biology, physiology and psychology required to succeed in my chosen discipline. I am fascinated by the various methods used to assess and measure physical activity and the changes in physiology that result from exercise and training. Last summer I attended a residential sports science summer school at my local university. We had various taster sessions with academics and I thoroughly enjoyed all of them. I was particularly fascinated by the Human Performance Unit because it was jam-packed with the latest gear. We were shown how all the different apparatus worked and were allowed to carry out tests using some of the more basic pieces. I also heard talks from current students and they really made me realise that I would fit into student life easily.

Sport is obviously very important to me and I do get involved both in and out of school. I play hockey at county level and will want to continue when I reach university. I am also eager to become involved in new sports and will enjoy helping to run clubs as I feel I have a lot of knowledge and experience to share. Football is also a strong passion of mine and I have recently been selected to assist with coaching the youth team at my town club. I am looking forward to working with children, as I know that I will gain lots of new skills.

I have a part-time job as a retail assistant in a leisure-wear shop. I really enjoy helping customers and advising them on the most appropriate clothing and equipment. I am also responsible for the tills at the end of the day and am often trusted to close the shop. I would consider myself to be an excellent communicator and I also possess good timekeeping skills; I hate being late for anything! I know that both these attributes will stand me in good stead for academic life.

I am so determined to become a student, studying the subject that I love. I know that I will put every effort into making the most of my time, both academically and socially.

Strengths:

✓ It is good to mention any previous experience of visiting universities, e.g. summer school or A level conference, as this demonstrates keen interest to the admissions tutor.

✓ This student backs up his interest in sport through a lot of extra-curricular involvement, which will be impressive to the admissions tutor.

Weaknesses:

✗ Although this student is clearly focused on the subject and has a sporting interest that is very important for his chosen subject area, he fails to present himself as a well-rounded person and is also slightly vague about what his career in sport will be.

✗ The final statement is slightly weak and would have been more effective if the student had summed up by reiterating the reasons why he is looking forward to going to university to study sports science.

 TOP TIPS

1 An interesting opening paragraph which goes straight to the point

2 Enthusiasm for the study of sports science and an understanding of the subject at degree level

3 Giving information about extra-curricular activities and skills gained through them

4 An interest in sport- and exercise-related activities outside the classroom

5 An awareness of the rigours of higher-level studying and independent learning

6 The ability to work well in practical classes and labs, as well as written and research skills

 THINGS TO AVOID

1 Spelling and punctuation mistakes – get your statement proofread carefully

2 Outdated information – sporting activities from primary school are not relevant

3 An interest in sport that does not go beyond watching it on TV

4 Exaggerated claims – tell us about your achievements but don't make them up

5 Giving too much information about your social activities and hobbies – focus on information relevant to your intended courses

 RECOMMENDED READING

▶ D. Sewell, P. Watkins and M. Griffin, *Sport and Exercise Science: An Introduction*, Routledge, 2012

I am grateful to the University of Essex for its help in preparing this profile. Other highly rated courses can be found at the universities of Bath, Bournemouth, Loughborough, Leeds and Birmingham.

THEATRE AND PERFORMANCE DESIGN AND TECHNOLOGY

This academic profile was written by admissions tutors at the Liverpool Institute of Performing Arts (LIPA). The information is useful to all applicants, but some of the advice is pertinent to that department in particular.

SUBJECT OVERVIEW

The theatre and entertainment industries have a lot of employees who have never studied at university, and some areas, such as the live sound industry, are keen that all new staff start at the bottom and work their way up – so why would you want to study a degree before starting employment? At university, you could learn a broad base of skills as a technician or designer to give you the flexibility to work in a number of environments, whereas an employer might initially want you for a specific task and not give you the opportunities to try new tasks. You may not need to start at the very bottom as a graduate, and, even if you do, you are much more likely to rise a lot faster. You may also hit a 'glass ceiling' as a non-graduate where some organisations will offer their more senior positions only to applicants with a degree.

WHAT SKILLS OR ATTRIBUTES DO ADMISSIONS TUTORS LOOK FOR IN A GOOD APPLICANT?

Academically, we are looking for people with five GCSE passes at a minimum grade of C or above, including English. In terms of Level 3 qualifications we don't specify which subjects you need to study – we are looking for people who achieve a minimum of 64 UCAS Tariff points, which should ideally be attained in one of the following ways:

- Grade C and C at A level or AVCE level. All A level subjects accepted, excluding general studies
- Merit, Pass, Pass Profile at BTEC National Diploma level.

All equivalent UK and overseas qualifications are also accepted, including Scottish Highers, Welsh, European and International Baccalaureate and Irish Leaving Certificate. These requirements will differ depending on the university and course.

For the design degree, we normally expect applicants to also successfully complete a Foundation studies course in art and design or an equivalent course at pre-degree level.

We are also interested in your experience to date in the subject, your interdisciplinary interest, your communication skills and enterprise.

In terms of personality traits, we look for people who are excited about studying the subject. A hunger to learn more and keep learning as your career goes on is important to us. You do not necessarily have to be an expert because, if you are, you may have nothing left to learn. You need to be good at talking about your own experience and what you have learnt from it and good at analysing your own strengths and weaknesses. You do not have to be perfect – what could we add to that?

A good sense of humour helps – you can be working for long hours, often under pressure, with lots of different personalities. You do not have to be a show-off but you must not be afraid to speak your mind. You will need some kind of independence to take on this degree course and must not be afraid to ask questions if you do not understand something (much better than pretending that you do know something when you don't).

You do not have to be a happy, smiley person about everything – but if you come in and complain about the course you're on at the moment, or things you have done in the past, you may come across as a negative person who may struggle to enjoy anything. Your enthusiasm should show itself in being able to describe what you like in a variety of different ways.

WHAT DOES A GOOD PERSONAL STATEMENT LOOK LIKE?

You need to show enthusiasm, coupled with a clear idea of where you want to go in the future and why this type of course might help you to get there or narrow-down your choices. It will help if you explain why studying at university is important, as well as why you just want to study the subject itself.

Example from a good personal statement

At the moment I'm on an art Foundation course and have a big interest in 3-D design and often try to combine my techniques from all areas, using my knowledge of structure to design and make extravagant garments. I especially enjoy working on combining materials such as wire, metal and wood with fabric. I have learnt how to manipulate material in different ways. I like experimenting with different techniques to produce different looks. I have had the opportunity to work in a wide variety of materials and styles and have been encouraged to be more creative and independent in my work. In my courses I particularly enjoy 'realisation', where I actually make my final design. It is the most exciting section of the coursework. And also the design process where I illustrate and explore media to record ideas. It is very satisfying when you can see how you have come to produce this final item. I find contextual studies very interesting, as I get a chance to explore and admire other artists' work, observing how their work relates to things around us. During these last two years of my studies I have built up a knowledge of other artists, in particular in my third year I have begun to create a personal sketch book of information and creativity of artists whose work inspires me by visiting galleries and other sources.

✓ In this statement, the applicant describes what s/he is doing now with enthusiasm and talks about developing these skills further in ways that are relevant to our course.

One of the main reasons why a personal statement might not work for us would be if the candidate appears to be torn between two different career paths. For example, if you are applying to acting or directing courses and are also applying to a design/technology course that suggests you might not be all that committed to our course. Being a designer or technician is a career in itself and we want to know you are committed to that – not to see it as a pathway to a career in performing. In one personal statement someone commented that they were really looking forward to 'retail display design'. This is not the course that they are applying for at LIPA. Similarly, another candidate spoke about their love of teaching and the fact that they really want to work with primary school children. That is not part of our course, so that candidate is more likely to be better placed studying a focused educational degree. We do have some students whose career aspirations change while studying, but if you already know before starting university that you'd rather do something else, then that's what you should be looking for in the courses you apply to.

 ## TOP TIPS

These tips are from a student who is studying Theatre and Performance Design at LIPA

1 Get involved both in school and outside of school if you can (try to explore opportunities to take part in local theatre) – this will enable you to write about these experiences in the personal statement and sell your genuine interest in the subject

2 Talk to people – both those who work on stage and backstage, about what happens behind the scenes.

 ## THINGS TO AVOID

1 Complaining that you haven't had any opportunities up till now – life is what you make it. A good personal statement needs to reflect the fact that you have done interesting things, so start now!

2 Thinking that musical theatre in the West End is the only successful or interesting type of show going on

3 Being an anorak – having a passion for something is more relevant to us than knowing every serial number or model number

Their experiences and what you learnt from them can also provide vital evidence of your interest. Put this in your statement

3 Try everything once – even if you don't carry on working on that element of the production in the future. Being able to understand everything that goes on in a theatre helps in the future. This willingness to try and not being afraid to ask is something that you should allude to in the statement and any interview you may be asked to attend

4 Watch shows and performances – that is what you will work towards, so it is always good and satisfying to see the final results. If you see a show and want to comment about the set design in the statement, this would be good

6 Draw, take photos and keep your show programmes. Keep a record of everything you do, otherwise you have got nothing to show for it. Bring this to any interview you may have

4 Concentrating your design work into fashionable or niche areas such as pictures of fairies or angels – try to show the breadth of your interest and a range of different applications in the statement or portfolio you bring to interview

5 Poor spelling, grammar and punctuation. This is just lazy and shows that you are not really serious. If in doubt, get your statement and application proofread by a good teacher, tutor or friend

 RECOMMENDED READING AND WEBSITES

- Alison Oddey, *The Potentials of Spaces: The Theory of Practice of Scenography & Performance*, University of Chicago Press, 2006
- Society of British Theatre Designers: www.theatredesign.org.uk
- Design Council: www.designcouncil.org.uk
- Broadcasting, Entertainment, Cinematograph and Theatre Union: www.bectu.org.uk

I am grateful for the support I received from the Liverpool Institute of Performing Arts (www.lipa.ac.uk) in the preparation of this profile. Other highly rated courses can be found at the universities of Edge Hill, Canterbury Christ Church and Bath Spa.

TOURISM MANAGEMENT

This academic profile was written by an admissions tutor at the University of Surrey's School of Hospitality and Tourism Management. The information is useful to all applicants, but some of the advice is pertinent to Surrey in particular.

SUBJECT OVERVIEW

Tourism is an activity of increasing economic significance in the world and makes important contributions to Gross National Product (GNP), employment, foreign currency earnings and employment. It also has both positive and negative social and environmental impacts and can contribute to poverty reduction. Because of this, universities have increasingly become interested in the management and understanding of tourism.

WHAT SKILLS OR ATTRIBUTES DO ADMISSIONS TUTORS LOOK FOR IN A GOOD APPLICANT?

There are no specific academic subjects that are prerequisites for studying tourism. More important are an interest and passion for the subject and evidence that you can benefit from a university course. The industry stereotype is for extrovert, fun-loving personality types – but there are also many opportunities for more introverted, studious applicants!

Clearly the teaching styles will vary from department to department; however, at Surrey we would expect to offer contact time of 12–18 hours per week. As the subject is relatively new, teaching and learning styles tend to be dynamic and innovative. Many courses include a field trip abroad. Assessment is generally mixed, including exams, coursework, projects and group work.

WHAT DOES A GOOD PERSONAL STATEMENT LOOK LIKE?

A good personal statement has a clear structure, with an introduction, a number of clearly explained and relevant points and a conclusion. It is well written, with correct grammar and spelling and without repetition. It effectively links your background, achievements, experience and interests to the course for which you have applied and it shows that you have undertaken some research into the subject area and into the nature of education at university level. It also shows that you have wider interests and achievements than those solely related to the course for which you have applied, and ideally you should show that you have critical and analytical abilities.

With these in mind the structure is likely to include:

- information about you and your interests and ambitions
- your present studies and how these relate to your study and longer-term ambitions
- your particular achievements
- your broad understanding and knowledge of your planned field of study
- why you are interested in it
- how you feel you would contribute to the field
- critical awareness of an issue or issues related to tourism and an ability to analyse the issue.

 TOP TIPS

1 Make sure that your statement has a clear structure with an introduction, a number of clearly explained and relevant points, and a conclusion

2 Have clear goals and state them clearly

3 Your statement must be well written, with correct grammar and spelling and without repetition

4 Link your background, achievements, experience and interests to the course for which you have applied, and show that you have undertaken some research into the subject area and into the nature of education at university level

5 You must also show that you have wider interests and achievements than those solely related to the course for which you have applied and, ideally, you should show that you have critical and analytical abilities

 THINGS TO AVOID

1 Poor spelling, punctuation and grammar

2 A statement that lacks clarity and direction

3 A statement that does not refer to your academic skills and extra-curricular interests

4 A statement that shows little evidence of an understanding of business and the tourism industry in general

RECOMMENDED READING AND WEBSITES

- The Tourism Society: www.tourismsociety.org
- Institute of Travel and Tourism: www.itt.co.uk
- Tourism Management Institute: www.tmi.org.uk
- VisitBritain: www.visitbritain.org

I am grateful to the department at the University of Surrey (www.surrey.ac.uk) for its support in compiling this profile. Other highly rated courses can be found at the universities of Bath Spa, Brighton, Exeter, Kent and Liverpool John Moores.

VETERINARY SCIENCE

This academic profile was written by an admissions tutor at the University of Nottingham Veterinary School. It was updated and new information included from other sources. The information is pertinent to all applicants but please be aware that some advice is relevant to Nottingham alone.

SUBJECT OVERVIEW

Studying veterinary medicine and science will allow you to gain the professionally recognised qualification that will allow you to practise as a veterinary surgeon. Making the decision to become a veterinary surgeon will set you on a course for one of the most varied and exciting careers available.

Only seven institutions offer veterinary medicine in the UK – Bristol, Cambridge, Edinburgh, Glasgow, Liverpool, London (Royal Veterinary College) and Nottingham. Competition is high, but it is a myth that you need to be exceptionally academic.

A veterinary medicine and science degree provides an excellent platform for a variety of careers. Graduates develop the in-depth scientific knowledge that underpins clinical veterinary practice. These skills will open up a wide range of career options, including veterinary clinical practice, research, pathology, conservation medicine, pharmaceutical industry, state veterinary medicine, food security, veterinary public health and policy.

Notice for students applying to Cambridge or the Royal Veterinary College
For all students who are currently applying for places on the veterinary degrees at either Cambridge or the Royal Veterinary College: please remember to register for

the Biomedical Admissions Test (BMAT), as it is a requirement for each of these universities. The University of Cambridge Local Examinations Syndicate (UCLES) has issued a reminder that 'students who don't take the BMAT won't receive an admissions interview'.

Veterinary Nursing (BSc)

Many other universities offer a degree in veterinary nursing. Veterinary nurses are trained to support the work of vets in practice and they enjoy good employment prospects. Entry requirements for these courses is less academic than for the veterinary science courses. Middlesex University offers a good course with a CCC entry, including biology.

WHAT SKILLS OR ATTRIBUTES DO ADMISSIONS TUTORS LOOK FOR IN A GOOD APPLICANT?

Academically, you should be able to show good overall achievement at GCSE level, including high grades in science subjects.

Biology must usually be offered at A level. The requirement for other subjects varies a little from university to university, but either one or two subjects from chemistry, physics or mathematics should be offered. Some universities may accept a third A level in a non-science subject, but it must be an academically sound subject. The minimum grades generally expected are AAB, though some schools will require AAA.

There are now other entry routes into vet school, including the preliminary year at Nottingham (which accepts students with high grades in non-science or vocational subjects). There are also widening participation courses specifically aimed at learners from under-represented groups, such as the Gateway course run at the Royal Veterinary College and Veterinary Science Certificate course at Lincoln (for progression to Nottingham) – these courses generally look for grades CCC at A2.

As a vet you will need good communication skills – listening, writing and speaking – and motor skills such as good hand–eye co-ordination, dexterity and precision. All vet schools will expect you to have gained some animal-focused work experience, preferably in a range of animal-related areas such as at a veterinary practice, working with horses or on a farm, at a zoo or wildlife park, in research or laboratory settings and spending time at an abattoir. You would be expected to have an understanding of the positive and negative aspects of a veterinary career and have an awareness of current important issues and developments in veterinary medicine and science.

It is important that you possess a number of personal attitudes and attributes that are needed to be successful both on the course and in a veterinary career, including a caring ethos (compassion, tolerance, patience, empathy) and a sense of social responsibility. You should be able to cope with change and uncertainty and to overcome challenges, while understanding your own limitations. Schools expect applicants to possess self-motivation, self-confidence, self-reliance and initiative. You should be able to show that you have the ability to work independently and as part of a team, integrate, co-operate and be flexible. Good personal organisational skills and time-management skills are a must.

WHAT DOES A GOOD PERSONAL STATEMENT LOOK LIKE?

A good personal statement will cover why you want to study veterinary medicine and science, detail your experience gained to date and your understanding of the profession. Admissions tutors will like to see some evidence of work experience where you came into contact with animals. This needs to be at least two weeks in length and references may be taken.

Taster courses such as Vet-Medlink are popular, useful but not obligatory. Mention the aspects of your A levels (or equivalent) that you have found particularly interesting. Describe any coursework you have completed and any books that you have read that may be relevant. Please do not lie, as this will become clear at interview!

Your statement should cover personal responsibilities and leadership, and any achievements and awards won, and an indication of how these relate to competences required of a veterinary surgeon. Needless to say, structure and organisation, grammar and spelling are also important.

Although your personal statement is important, most schools will have additional methods of assessment including the Biomedical Admissions Test (BMAT – www.bmat.org), online questionnaires and work experience references.

 TOP TIPS

1 Say why you want to study veterinary medicine and science

2 Detail your experience gained to date and your understanding of the profession

 THINGS TO AVOID

1 Having a rose-tinted picture of the profession – it will include working at night, in all conditions, and you will be paid as much as a medic! Show that you understand this in your statement and interview

3 Emphasise the work experience early on and explain what you learnt as well as what you did

4 Taster courses such as Vet-Medlink are popular and useful but not obligatory

5 Mention the aspects of your A levels (or equivalent) that you have found particularly interesting

6 Include personal responsibilities and leadership, and any achievements and awards won, and an indication of how these relate to the competences required of a veterinary surgeon

2 Poor spelling, grammar and punctuation

RECOMMENDED READING AND WEBSITES

- James Barton, *Getting into Veterinary School*, Trotman Education, 2015
- A. Shepherd, *Careers Working with Animals*, 9th edition, Kogan Page, 2001
- The Nerdy Vet's Vet School Success: www.vetschoolsuccess.com/chris-the-nerdy-vet
- Royal College of Veterinary Surgeons: www.rcvs.org.uk produces a free leaflet called 'Training to be a Veterinary Surgeon'
- British Veterinary Association: www.bva.co.uk
- British Veterinary Nursing Association: www.bvna.org.uk
- People's Dispensary for Sick Animals: www.pdsa.org.uk

I am grateful to the University of Nottingham Veterinary School (www.nottingham.ac.uk/vet) for its support in compiling this profile.

PART THREE
FURTHER INFORMATION

If you walk into any good bookshop, or careers library, you will see a vast array of books aimed at helping applicants to apply for university. This is one such book! There are also books that offer advice about budgeting, cooking, essay writing and gap years. Trotman are one of the UK's leading Careers and HE publishers and the following list shows the range of books on offer. I have also included websites, as these are a growing source of information.

This is not an exhaustive list. New books are written and websites created every month. Some are expensive and perhaps worth browsing in a library. Others are cheaper and worth buying yourself.

WHAT SHOULD I STUDY GUIDES

Trotman and other publishers produce a wide range of regularly updated books that help you to choose the course you want to study – here are some of the latest books by Trotman Education that I recommend you look at:

Choosing Your Degree Course and University
Getting into Oxford and Cambridge
Getting into Medical School
Getting into Art & Design Courses
Getting into Physiotherapy Courses
Getting into Law
Getting into Psychology Courses
Getting into Business & Economics Courses
Getting into Dental School
Getting into Engineering Courses
Getting into Veterinary School
Getting into Nursing and Midwifery Courses
Getting into Pharmacy & Pharmacology Courses

GOOD UNIVERSITY GUIDES

There are many of these guides in the bookshops or online. Some are better than others, and below you will find my personal recommendations.

The Times Good University Guide, Times Books
This is updated annually and is available online. Although formal in style, it does offer sound and unbiased advice.

Other good online starting points are The Complete University Guide or UNISTATS. Both can be 'Googled' easily.

The *Guardian* also runs a very good online university guide.

ALTERNATIVE PROSPECTUSES

Many universities now produce alternative prospectuses and guides. These are written by students, for students and are not always endorsed by the college authorities. While they will promote the university, they also offer an insight into the day-to-day life of a student that you will not find elsewhere.

These guides are available online. Use a search engine to find them. Most universities now use social networks too, with Facebook and Twitter sites.

However, one site that offers a 'one-stop shop' approach is www.whatuni.com, where current students post comments about the university where they are studying.

GENERAL GUIDES TO SUBJECTS AND COURSE REQUIREMENTS

HEAP: University Degree Course Offers, Trotman Education
This book is one of the best-known in the higher education world. By Brian Heap, it is annually updated and is the most comprehensive single source for subject-specific information available. Students can find out about and research a range of subjects, including offers most commonly made by each university, information about interviews, open days and the number of applicants who apply per place. This is an expensive book to buy, so probably look at this in your library.

The content is also available online at www.heaponline.co.uk; your school can subscribe to the website.

How to Complete Your UCAS Application, Trotman Education
This guide offers support on choosing what to study and the complete application process – from important deadlines, to succeeding at interviews and navigating the UCAS Apply system.

APPLICATIONS OVERSEAS

This is a new and growing market for UK students, particularly to mainland Europe. These two websites offer an insight into what this involves:

www.topuniversities.com
www.studyineurope.eu

Books that are good include:

Studying Abroad, Trotman Education

OTHER GUIDES

Finally, the quirky books about food, taking a gap year or budgeting.

A Guide to Uni Life, Trotman

Cut the Cost of Uni, Trotman

Your Gap Year, Trotman

Work Your Way Around the World, Trotman

Teaching English Abroad, Trotman